D1082499

Act I, Scene 1
Set designed by Darwin Reid Payne
Photograph by Butch Nevius

A Christmas Carol

Dramatized by Darwin Reid Payne

From a short story by Charles Dickens

Southern Illinois University Press

Carbondale and Edwardsville

Printed in the United States of America

Designed by Richard Hendel

Photographs by Butch Nevious

Library of Congress Cataloging in
Publication Data

Payne, Darwin Reid.
     A Christmas carol.

     SUMMARY: A dramatized version of the
tale in which a miser learns the true
meaning of Christmas when three ghostly
visitors review his life and forecast his
future.
     1. Christmas plays. [1. Christmas
plays. 2. Plays] I. Dickens, Charles,
1812-1870. Christmas carol. II. Title.
PS3566.A9365C5   1981   812'.54   80-18827
ISBN 0-8093-0999-8

For Gene Penland

PREFACE

In the year 1843 Charles Dickens wrote <u>A</u>
<u>Christmas</u> <u>Carol</u>. From the beginning it
captured the imagination of all who read
it. Shortly after the story was printed,
Ebenezer Scrooge stepped off the page and
on to the stage. At first it was Dickens
himself who brought Scrooge into the
theater; his readings--first for his family
and friends and later for the general
public--made Scrooge as important a
dramatic creation as he had been a
fictional character. But the immense
popularity of Scrooge's strange tale with
its awesome nightmare visions increasingly
demanded greater scope and more lavish
presentation. Numerous dramatizations soon
appeared in theaters the world over. Most
of these adaptations have now vanished;
few, in fact, were ever published. Even
today the number of full-length versions
of the play in print is small although the
popularity of the story has never been
greater.

This adaptation of <u>A</u> <u>Christmas</u> <u>Carol</u>
is intended for those who desire a play of
reasonable length but not of unreasonable
production demands. While supernatural
effects certainly induce audiences to
attend the play, I hope that the interplay
of characters as presented here will be
equally attractive. I have taken no great
liberties with the original story; while
some changes were necessary for dramatic
purpose, I made a real attempt to preserve
as much of Dickens's story as possible.
Although the characters in the original
tale are numerous (and some did not make

the transition), the actual number of performers needed to act this play does not exceed eighteen or twenty; the sequence of scenes, some fourteen in all, are not overly elaborate. I recommend simplicity.

Actually there are only three basic requirements for the successful presentation of any of Dickens's works adapted for dramatic purposes. The first requirement is to make a sincere attempt to show the living people Dickens created as they moved through their own time and world, not to broadly paint them as simple caricatures. His creations are often full-blown and grotesque, their actions large and eccentric; but they are, nonetheless, true reflections of the life he saw around him and, more important, real.

The second requirement is to assure that the actions of the story be performed with the same brisk tautness with which Dickens wrote them; a certain sweep and momentum in the work must be observed constantly. The pace of any production is of great importance; speed alone, however, will not assure that the proper flow of action has been achieved. It is also important to understand that A Christmas Carol is a phantasmagorical vision; each scene melts into the next, sometimes imperceptively, sometimes with spasmodic intensity. Dream, nightmare, and reality constantly interchange; awareness of these transformations is essential and must be made clear to an audience. In order to follow the author's intent, the action of the play must be as continuous as possible.

The third requirement--and by no means the least important--is to realize that Scrooge's London in A Christmas Carol

is much like that of Prospero's island in
The Tempest: both are places "full of
strange noises." In both, the aural is as
essential to a successful production as is
appropriate setting or costume; the role
that sound plays in this particular
version, moreover, cannot be overemphasized.
Nor can the kinds and qualities of the
individual sounds required be too little
considered. While the directions that
accompany the text give some indication as
to what is necessary to create the aural
background of Scrooge's dream (and, it
should be mentioned that the continuity of
sound during the entire play is also
extremely important) a careful reading of
the text will show just how pervasive and
critical this aspect of the production is.
In the original performances most of the
sound was "live": bells of various pitches
and tonal size, gongs, chimes, chains,
iron bars, moans, winds, subterranean
rumbles, and--not least--the orchestrated
choral sounds of offstage actors were
constantly added to and mixed with all the
other sounds. (While carols appear in
several instances during the performance,
only the Second Spirit's entrance music is
given at the end of the text.) Although
taped or recorded sound can be employed, a
precise orchestration of effects is less
possible without the subtle interplay of
live sound and live performer.
     Floor plans for individual scenes and
other production data--property, costume,
and light plots--have been omitted from
this script. Individual theaters and
individual producing groups so vary in
their resources and staff composition that
I feel such information would be of little
real value. More importantly, however,

there is no absolutely "right" way of producing a play from this script; while production suggestions are incorporated into the text's directions they in no way preclude other approaches. Dickens was an adventurous writer; we should be no less so in our bringing his creations to the stage.

Carbondale, Illinois   Darwin Reid Payne
June 1980

A CHRISTMAS CAROL

SYNOPSIS OF SCENES

ACT I

ACT II

The action of the play takes place in the city of London.

The time is Christmas eve and Christmas morning of the year 1843.

This play was first produced by The University Theater, Southern Illinois University at Carbondale during December 1979.

CAST OF CHARACTERS

Ebenezer Scrooge

Bob Cratchit

Mr. Boswell

Mr. Johnson

Scrooge's Nephew

A Beggar

The Ghost of Marley

The Spirit of
Christmas Past

Fezziwig

Mrs. Fezziwig

Young Ebenezer

Dick Wilkins

A Fiddler

The Spirit of
Christmas Present

Peter Cratchit

Belinda Cratchit

Mrs. Cratchit

Tiny Tim

Martha Cratchit

The Spirit of
Christmas Yet to Come

An Old Crone

An Old Man

First Businessman

Second Businessman

Boy

(Carolers, Dancers, Attendants to the
Second Spirit, Citizens of London)

ACT I

SCENE I
A street in London during the middle
of the last century. It is early
evening of Christmas eve. Bells ring
from various quarters of the city.
Late shoppers hurriedly pass through
the streets on last minute errands
before the closing of the shops. A
small group of carolers can be heard
faintly in some side street, their
song becoming stronger as they
approach. Finally they appear and
stop outside one of the offices which
line the street, this being part of
the commercial section of London. The
song of the carolers, the softly
falling snow and the progress of the
lamplighter as he goes from street
lantern to street lantern creates the
near-perfect image of an English
Christmas season many years ago.

CAROLERS
God rest you merry gentlemen,
Let nothing you dismay.
Remember Christ our Savior
Was born on Christmas day,
To save us all from Satan's power
When we have gone astray.
Oh, tidings of comfort and joy, comfort
    and joy,
Oh, tidings of comfort and joy. . . .

SCROOGE
(Suddenly appearing at a window above the
Caroler's heads.) What!? Is the town on
fire!? Speak! Is some great and terrible
calamity fallen on us!?

                              The surprized singers
                              look first at him and
                              then at one another.
                              Finally, a small boy
                              steps forward.

                    TINY TIM
No, Mr. Scrooge. Not that we know of.

                    SCROOGE
Oh? Then, pray, Master Noise-Maker, what
means this caterwaul in the streets while
serious and sober men are still at honest
work!?

                    BELINDA
It's Christmas eve, Mr. Scrooge.

                    SCROOGE
Eh!?

                    BELINDA
It's Christmas eve, sir. We thought you
would want a Christmas song.

                    SCROOGE
(Rudely mimicking her.) Oh, you thought I
would want a Christmas song, did ye!?

                    ALL
Yes, sir.

                    BELINDA
(Losing confidence as she speaks.) We
thought you might.

                    SCROOGE
(Explosively.) Well, you thought me wrong!
I do not want--I do not need--any song of
any sort! Last of all a Christmas song!
(He pronounces Christmas as if it were a

4   Act I

filthy word.) What I do want, now the
subject's raised, is a little quiet outside
me own office. Nor do I have time to hang
from windows hearing winter-wastrels foul
the air with Christmas noise. Now be off!!!

                    PETER
But, sir--It is Christmas eve. . . .

                    SCROOGE
And what means that!? Is it a day more to
be wasted than others? No, impertinent
fellow! It's a day, that's what it is! A
whole day. And days were meant for honest
labor! All of 'em--every one! The world
does not run round on Christmas eves. Now,
for the last time, off with you all before
I call down the law on each and every
one!!! Off, I say!

                              Sadly the carolers
                              turn away and start
                              down the street. After
                              a few steps, the small
                              girl turns back:

                    BELINDA
All the same, Mr. Scrooge, a Merry
Christmas to you and yours.

                    SCROOGE
BAH! HUMBUG!!!

                              The carolers resume
                              their song and their
                              journey.

Bah! . . . a plague on your Merry
Christmases . . . fools . . . wastrels.

SCENE 2
He slams the window shut, the
carolers continuing down the street.
The office opens as Scrooge steps
down from the window. His clerk, Bob
Cratchit, who has been watching
Scrooge with a pained expression
quickly resumes his work as Scrooge
turns toward him.

And you!

                    CRATCHIT
Sir?

                    SCROOGE
If I want disapproving looks from my
clerks, I'll pay for 'em! I don't want
them gratis! Do we have an understanding!?

                    CRATCHIT
(Meekly.) Yes, sir. I understand.

                    SCROOGE
(As he irritates a pile of papers.) I hope
you do, sir. I sincerely hope you do.

                              He rubs his hands and
                              looks toward the small
                              stove that serves to
                              warm the office.

And fetch a coal for the fire.

                              Looking back at the
                              window.

Not only are they fools, it costs me heat
to tell 'em so.

                    CRATCHIT
Yes, sir. At once.

                    SCROOGE
(Quickly.) But only one coal, mind! I'm not
made of money. (To himself.) Though every
idler seems to think it.

                         Scrooge resumes his
                         seat at his own desk.
                         Down the outside
                         street two older well-
                         dressed men appear.
                         They stop before the
                         office of Scrooge and
                         consult a list one
                         carries. Both nod and,
                         after a moment, ring
                         the pull bell on the
                         door. Scrooge does not
                         stir. When the men
                         receive no answer, the
                         bell is rung a second
                         time.

Come in! We have no footmen here to attend
doors! If you want inside you'll open your
own door!

                         The two men step
                         inside. After shaking
                         snow from their
                         clothes, they casually
                         examine the gloomy
                         ill-lit office. It is
                         immediately obvious
                         that while they are
                         imbued with the spirit

Scene 2   7

> of the day, little of
> that spirit exists
> here. Scrooge glares
> at both but does not
> move. Finally, one
> steps forward.

BOSWELL
Have I the pleasure, sir, of addressing
. . . (reading from the list). . . . Mr.
Jacob Marley, Esquire . . . or Mr.
Ebenezer Scrooge, Esquire?

SCROOGE
(Snorts.) A pretty trick if it were Jacob
Marley--(sneeringly) Esquire.

BOSWELL
I beg your pardon?

SCROOGE
(Pointing to a picture of Marley on the
wall above his head.) That--is Jacob
Marley--Esquire.

BOSWELL
And is he here?

SCROOGE
(Impatiently closes the ledger in front of
him.) Dead.

JOHNSON
Dead?

BOSWELL
Dead?

SCROOGE

Dead! Dead as dead is or can ever be. Dead
these seven years. Dead this very night,
to be precise.

BOSWELL

Our belated condolences, Mr. Scrooge. . . .

SCROOGE

(Rising.) Left me, he did, to deal with a
foolish world . . . (bitterly to himself)
. . . a foolish world. (Stepping toward
the men.) Well? You have business with me?
If so, be about it.

> Cratchit returns with
> a lump of coal.

Too big! Too big!! Break it in half.

> Cratchit obeys.

JOHNSON

Indeed, we did not know of Mr. Marley's
death. The sign outside your door says. . .

SCROOGE

New signs cost money! Needless expense. A
useless extravagance.

JOHNSON

(Exchanging a look with his partner.) Yes.
. . . Yes, quite so, my dear sir, quite
so. Our appologies. . . .

SCROOGE

(Impatiently.) You have business?

BOSWELL

Sir?

SCROOGE

(Beginning to lose his temper.) Business, sir! Business! Do you or do you not have business with me!? Or is it your custom to interrupt the business of others as some belated school-boy prank?

JOHNSON

(Forcing a smile.) Indeed, sir. We do have business with you. Very important business. One most important at this time of year.

SCROOGE

(Examining papers in his hand.) Then be about it.

JOHNSON

My friend and I, Mr. Boswell. . . .

BOSWELL

And my friend, Mr. Johnson. . . .

JOHNSON

. . . We spend each Christmas eve gathering from our merchant brothers some little from each so that the plight of the less fortunate may be made more bearable.

SCROOGE

Eh?

BOSWELL

To ease the burden of those afflicted with the winter's cruelties.

JOHNSON

We seek. . . .

SCROOGE

(Coldly interrupting.) And I seek, too, sir.

BOSWELL
I beg your pardon?

SCROOGE
I seek to make some meaning out of all
these fine and fuzzy phrases. The Business,
sirs! What is your business with me!?
Speak to the point or I must wish you a
good day and get back to my own business
which waits upon that desk and is not
getting done! Is that clearly spoken
enough for ye!?

JOHNSON
(Slightly irritated.) Very clear indeed,
Mr. Scrooge. All we would ask of you is a
small donation from your establishment to
aid the poor and needy who feel so keenly
the lack of that which we all have in
abundance.

SCROOGE
Speak for yourselves! Abundance? Nothing.
I have nothing to spare. Least of all time.
(He returns to his desk.) Good day. (His
bony finger pointing to the door.) The
same door that brought you in will serve
to see you out. (To himself.) Abundance,
indeed!

BOSWELL
(Incredulous.) Are we to understand that
so prosperous and respected a man as
yourself would not want to be represented
on the list?

SCROOGE
You understand most correctly. (He has
returned to his writing.)

JOHNSON
Surely your sympathy for the poor widow
and her pitiful child. . . .

SCROOGE
And have all the work-houses in England
closed their doors? Have they all gone out
of business? For if such be the case I
have not had the news.

BOSWELL
(Firmly, but sadly.) I wish to God I could
report it were so.

SCROOGE
Ah!? Then such places still be where your
poor and cold may go?

JOHNSON
(Softly.) Indeed, sir. They do still exist.

SCROOGE
Then there they must go.

JOHNSON
Many cannot; others would rather die.

SCROOGE
If they would rather die, then let them do
it. And decrease the surplus population.

BOSWELL
(More firmly.) Surely, sir. . . .

SCROOGE
(Forging ahead in his diatribe.) These
houses are kept open with my taxes, sir!
My money! Bled from me! Good money paid
out for those who will not earn their
bread as I attempt to do at this present

moment, were it not for
i n t e r r u p t i o n!

> The two men draw
> themselves up and
> prepare to leave.
> Just as they open the
> door, Mr. Johnson
> turns back to Scrooge.

                    JOHNSON
Nonetheless, sir, we wish you the tidings
of the season and hope you may someday see
fit to join our cause.

                    SCROOGE
Good day!!!

> The men leave. Distant
> carolers are heard
> singing It Came Upon
> A Midnight Clear. The
> evening has turned to
> night. Scrooge
> continues to shuffle
> papers as he mutters
> to himself.

. . . fools . . . fools. . . .

> Cratchit slowly shakes
> his head as he bends
> over his work. Now a
> jaunty striding figure
> appears at the office
> door. He tips his top
> hat to some passersby.
> Straightening his
> cravat and cuffs, he
> enters.

Scene 2   13

NEPHEW
Greetings of the season, Bob Cratchit! May
this be the best of many happy Christmas
times.

CRATCHIT
(Brightening, but still aware of Scrooge's
gaze.) And the very same to you, sir. The
very same to you!

NEPHEW
And make doubly sure those same good
wishes are delivered to your good wife and
family. (Looks at his watch.) But
certainly you should be there now? It's
Christmas eve, man, Christmas eve!

> Cratchit looks at the
> clock on the wall
> which says two
> o'clock.

But surely your clock has stopped. The
time is well past. . . .

SCROOGE
(Still writing.) The clock is broken,
nephew, and as useless as those who watch
it too closely.

NEPHEW
But, uncle, how does one tell the time
with a broken clock?

> He makes the question
> sound like a humorous
> riddle. But Scrooge
> will not be baited.

SCROOGE
The time, nephew, is what I say it is, and
I say there is none to waste in idle chat.
What is it you want? Be brief. Other fools
have been here before so I have no time to
waste on you.

NEPHEW
(Laughing as he always does at his
cantankerous relative.) Time, uncle, is
what I seem to have most.

SCROOGE
And I least. What's it you want?

NEPHEW
Why, nothing, uncle, except to deliver in
person a heartfelt invitation to you to
attend a gala affair. Where? (Slyly.) I
can detect your great impatience to know.
The answer: This very evening at the
apartments let by yours truly. On second
thought, "gala affair" may be too strong a
term. Let us merely say, a very good party
and a promisory note to pay great
entertainment to all who attend.

SCROOGE
Bah! Humbug! No time for such foolishness.

NEPHEW
I would be greatly honored to count you
among my guests. What say you, uncle, will
ye come?

SCROOGE
"Gala affairs." "Very good parties." Each
year the world goes mad on this one night.
. . . my own kin among 'em!

Scene 2   15

NEPHEW
But a fine madness, you must admit, uncle.
One I hoped you might come to share with
the rest of us poor benighted mortals.

SCROOGE
. . . Bah!

NEPHEW
I especially wanted you to attend this
evening since it is a very special day in
my life.

SCROOGE
So every fool would have you believe this
day is special.

NEPHEW
And so it is, uncle. But--and here I must
ask you to contain your natural
exhuberance--how many days in a man's life
does he become--BETHROTHED!? I ask you
that, uncle?

SCROOGE
Bethrothed!? You, without so much a ha-
penny to your credit?

                    He goes back to his
                    desk in disgust.

You're a greater fool, nephew, than I took
you for.

NEPHEW
(Not to be goaded on this happy day.)
Indeed, uncle, you have found me out. I am
just that very thing! A fool--but a fool
in love. In short, a happy fool. Perhaps
the happiest in all England.

SCROOGE
(Quickly.) In short, sir, a fool!

NEPHEW
Come, uncle! To be serious: as my only
living relative, I would very much have
you share my present happiness. And to
share that happiness with the dearest girl
in this or any other world, past, present
or future. That being, my sweetest wife to
be.

CRATCHIT
(Unable to restrain his true feelings.)
May I wish you the happiest of times, sir,
and the best of lives.

SCROOGE
(Sarcastically.) And may I wish you back
to the work on your desk!

CRATCHIT
(Instantly deflated.) Yes, sir. At once,
sir. . . .

NEPHEW
(Still good natured.) Uncle, uncle! Cast
off this morbid humor. The day, uncle.
Remember the day. It is true I do not have
at the moment, not to put too fine a point
on it, an excess of ready coin. (Scrooge
scoffs.) But . . . (his finger playfully
on the lapel of Scrooge) I consider the
sincere good wishes of others a treasure
beyond value. That is all I really desire
from you, good sir. (Turning to Cratchit.)
And my eternal debt to you for yours, Bob
Cratchit.

SCROOGE

May I take this occasion to remind you, young sir, you have debts enough. Your inheritance left in my keep is near run through. And a pretty penny it was at the start.

NEPHEW

Could there possibly be some error in the keeping of the books?

> He knows this will get a rise out of the old man, who prides himself on very accurate accounting practices. Even Cratchit is hard-pressed to keep from laughing at the jibe.

SCROOGE

Young scallywag! I can account for every penny you have thrown away, and well ye know it! (Thumping a ledger.) It is here! All here--every idle trip to the tailor, every wasted farthing!!

NEPHEW

(Brushing his near penury aside.) Tush, uncle. A trifle. What is important is that a new and greater treasure than any these mercantile walls could hold is about to be mine. And I would have you see her first-hand: a vision nonpareil! But say, uncle, jesting aside: will you share a cup with us this evening? (Slyly.) Costs nothing, uncle.

SCROOGE

(Turning aside.) Bah!

> Scrooge returns to his
> desk seeing there is
> no end to the
> conversation otherwise.
> A distant steeple bell
> begins to strike six.
> Cratchit stiffens
> since it tells how
> late the evening has
> become. The nephew
> takes out his pocket
> watch and shows it to
> Cratchit who nods
> sadly at the time.

NEPHEW

(Sighs.) Well, uncle Ebenezer, you cannot
say you have not been asked. And most
cordially too, you must admit. More than
that this poor fool cannot do. (Straightens
his cravat once more, adjusts his hat.)
Six o'clock and only half my errands run.

> He starts for the
> door.

A merry Christmas to you Bob Cratchit. Oh,
yes. . . .

> Takes a coin from his
> pocket and gives it to
> him.

This for Tiny Tim--a brave little lad.

CRATCHIT

Oh, thank you sir. This will be much
appreciated by Tim. The seasons greetings

to you and yours. (More softly so that
Scrooge does not hear.) And the very best
to your intended.

                    NEPHEW
(At the door.) You know the house, uncle.
May we hope to see you?

                    SCROOGE
(With measured tone.) When every fool who
goes about with Merry Christmas on his
lips has a stake of holly through his
heart and is cooked in his own plum
pudding. Then, nephew, and not a moment
before, ye may hope to see me! Not a
moment before. And close the door! I am
not paid to heat every alleyway in London!

                    NEPHEW
(Good naturedly.) Surely you cannot really
hold such sentiments, uncle.

                    SCROOGE
I do! I do! Now shut the door!!!

                         The nephew exists
                         laughing. Once out,
                         he steps to a front
                         window of the office
                         and taps on the
                         glass. When the two
                         in the office look up,
                         he tips his hat once
                         more in a gallant
                         gesture.

                    NEPHEW
A merry Christmas, uncle! And a very
prosperous New Year.

                              With this last salvo
                              delivered he continues
                              down the street
                              greeting every
                              passerby with high-
                              spirited good wishes.
                              Once again Scrooge
                              attempts to resume
                              his work. Cratchit
                              takes out his watch.
                              Gathering up his
                              courage, he carefully
                              closes the ledger in
                              front of him and
                              timidly approaches the
                              desk of Scrooge. He
                              stands waiting for
                              Scrooge's attention.
                              Scrooge continues to
                              write for a moment
                              more before taking
                              notice of his clerk.

                    SCROOGE
Well!?

                    CRATCHIT
I was wondering, sir. . . .

                    SCROOGE
(Impatiently.) Wondering? Wondering!?
What!? Out with it, man!

                    CRATCHIT
. . . if I might be allowed to leave a
little early this evening . . . being that
the day is. . . .

SCROOGE
(Cutting him off.) What time does this
establishment customarily shut its doors,
Mr. Cratchit?

CRATCHIT
(Slight hesitation.) . . . That would be
seven o'clock, Mr. Scrooge.

SCROOGE
(Holds up a large timepiece from the desk.)
And what, pray, do you read there?

CRATCHIT
(Slight pause.) . . . Only just gone six.

SCROOGE
(With heavy sarcasm.) Ohhhhh . . . then my
eyes do not deceive me? It does say only
six o'clock--not seven? Dear me! I thought
me mind was slipping into dotage . . .
that it might be seven after all and I had
somehow failed to notice how the time had
passed.

> Cratchit stands with
> head bowed. After a
> hard moment, Scrooge
> puts the watch back
> onto the desk.

It's plain to see I'll get no more work
from you this day. (With a wave of the
hand.) Go. Go! I've had enough of mortals
for one day.

CRATCHIT
(Instantly brightening.) Thank you. Thank
you, very much, Mr. Scrooge.

SCROOGE

(His pen scratching away.) . . . Fools.

CRATCHIT

(A step back to Scrooge.) If I might. . . .

SCROOGE

Now what is it?!

CRATCHIT

It being almost the end of the week, would
it be possible, do you think. . . .

SCROOGE

To have the wages not due for another whole
day? Is that it? Eh?!

CRATCHIT

Yes, sir.

SCROOGE

Your full wages, I suppose?

> Cratchit does not
> answer.

. . . And tomorrow off? That too, Mr.
Cratchit . . . that too!?

CRATCHIT

(Softly.) If convenient . . . as it is
Christmas day.

SCROOGE

No sir, it is not "convenient," as you say.
Not "convenient" at all. A fine excuse to
pick the pockets of honest men every three
hundred and sixty-fifth day, year in, year
out!

> Cratchit is again
> silent.

And always expected to pay the full wage
just as if the time had been worked out.

> Cratchit remains
> immobile.

Bah! (To himself.) Robbery. . . .

> With a self-righteous
> sigh, Scrooge takes a
> money box from out
> his desk and opens it
> with a key attached
> to a heavy gold chain
> which crosses his
> waistcoat. He counts
> out a small number of
> coins in a neat pile
> at the front of the
> desk. Pointing to the
> completed pile, he
> indicates that
> Cratchit may pick up
> his wage.

SCROOGE
There! I suppose there will be precious
little of that left after tomorrow.

CRATCHIT
Sir?

SCROOGE
Your Christmas doings! Your sugarplums and
other whatnot!

CRATCHIT
It is only once a year. The children do so look forward to the day.

SCROOGE
Well, see that you are here all the earlier the following day.

CRATCHIT
(Putting on his scarf and top hat.) Oh, that I will sir. That I will. And a joyful holiday, Mr. Scrooge.

SCROOGE
Humph! Robbed one moment and wished well the next! A "joyful holiday" indeed! Did you bed the fire, Mr. Cratchit?

CRATCHIT
(At the door.) The fire is out, sir.

SCROOGE
And not surprizing, what with the door continually flapped in the dead of winter.

CRATCHIT
(Almost free.) Yes, sir. Good night, Mr. Scrooge. And Merry. . . .

Scrooge cuts him off with a "Bah--Humbug" which cannot dampen the spirit of Cratchit at this moment. Stepping out into the cold evening air, Cratchit pauses, takes a deep breath and looks up at the sky. Seeing some very bright star, the burden of the office seems to fall from his shoulders. Straightening up, he gives a good jingle to the coins in his hand and starts down the street. A small girl selling apples approaches him. She is dressed in ragged clothes and looks underfed. He signals kindly that he does not want to buy. After a few steps he reconsiders, goes back and holds out a small coin. She gives him an apple and a grateful smile. He pats her head and resumes his progress down the street. Distant bells are heard. Scrooge, who has been bent over his papers all this while, closes the ledgers in front of him with sudden impatience.

SCROOGE
The world's a mad improvident place!
Nothing but fools and fools with nothing.
Yet each year they prance and sing and
make even greater fools of themselves
than the year before. (Shakes his head.)
A mad place . . . a humbug. . . .

A steeple clock bell
strikes seven. Scrooge
rises, takes out his
watch and looks at it.
With slow fussiness
he begins to put the
office in order for
the night. First he
turns out the dim
lamps. Next he goes
to the stove, stirs
the dead ashes and
puts the poker beneath
it. Going back to his
desk he puts away the
ledgers on their
proper shelves.
Something troubles
him, yet he cannot
seem to bring the
problem into focus.
He stands distractedly
at his desk for a
brief time before
shaking himself out
of his melancholy
reverie.

A mad place . . . a foolish mad place. . . .

He puts on his scarf,
cloak, and top hat.
He hesitates a moment
and then looks up at
the picture of Marley.
The wind blows through
the alleyway; there
seems to be low
moaning voices in it.

And you left me to deal with it alone,
Jacob Marley. Left me to bear the burden.
Well, you would be the last to say I
haven't done well. I've minded the
business, Jacob. I've minded it well.
You're a rich man . . . dead though ye
be. Rich. . . .

> A ghostly voice
> floats on the wind.

VOICE
Have-you-minded-the-business-of-the-world-
Ebenezer-Scrooge?

SCROOGE
Eh!? What's that?

> The voice speaks
> again, but softer and
> more distant than
> before.

VOICE
Have-you-minded-the-business-of-human-
kind . . . Eb-be-ne-zer-Scroooooge. . . .

SCROOGE
(A breathless moment.) Nothing . . . a
creaking old place . . . wind down some
long cracked chimney . . . nothing . . .
nothing more . . . only the wind. . . .

> SCENE 3
> He locks the door, steps out into the
> street, and, like Bob Cratchit, looks
> up at the sky. But, unlike Bob
> Cratchit, the view he sees weighs him
> down: nothing but black winter
> overhead. Shuddering, he pulls his

coat tighter about him and begins his
treck toward his own doorstep. The
wind rises to a higher level. The
streets are completely empty. A dark
figure emerges from the shadows of an
alleyway. It touches Scrooge on the
arm. Scrooge turns to see an old lame
beggar.

                    BEGGAR
Sir. . . .?

                    SCROOGE
Eh!? (Pulling back.) What do'ye want!? Be
off!

                    BEGGAR
It is a bitter cold night.

                    SCROOGE
(Turns to leave.) Then get you to a warmer
place . . . leave me be.

                    BEGGAR
Your pity, sir! A small coin could buy me
a night's shelter.

                         The man catches at
                         Scrooge's sleeve more
                         forcefully. Scrooge
                         pulls away in disgust.

                    SCROOGE
Take your hand from me!

                    BEGGAR
(Still holding onto Scrooge.) Sir. . . .

                    SCROOGE
At once, I say!!!

                    BEGGAR
Only a penny, sir. . . . Even a ha-penny.

                    SCROOGE
And I say <u>get</u> <u>you</u> <u>away</u> <u>from</u> <u>me</u>!

                              The beggar stares at
                              him a moment.

                    BEGGAR
Nothing?

                    SCROOGE
(With venom.) Nothing!!!

                              The beggar turns away
                              and disappears into
                              the shadows muttering
                              to himself.

                    BEGGAR
Nothing . . . no pity . . . nothing. . . .

                              The wind rises as
                              Scrooge makes his way
                              through the empty
                              streets. Suddenly he
                              stops and looks
                              behind him; he is
                              certain he has heard
                              his name being called.

                    SCROOGE
Eh?! Who's there? (No reply.) Nothing . . .
the trick of a tired mind. Nothing . . .
nothing more.

                              He continues to his
                              own house.

VOICE OF MARLEY

Eb-be-ne-zer-Scrooooooooooge. . . .

> Startled, he drops
> the key in his hand
> on the door stoop.
> When he rises from
> picking it up, he is
> horrified to see, in
> the great knocker on
> his door, the face of
> Jacob Marley. As he
> gazes dumbstruck at
> the vision, the closed
> eyes of the face very
> slowly open. Scrooge
> reels back; the vision
> fades. The door
> knocker is as it had
> always been.

SCROOGE

Nothing . . . a trick of a tired mind . . .
only that. . . .

SCENE 4

He unlocks the door and quickly
enters. As he does, the house opens
to reveal the sitting room of Scrooge.
It is as gaunt and cheerless as
Scrooge himself. A bleak, cold place
without warmth of any kind. At the
back is a massive single door with
several large boltlocks as well as
the customary keyhole lock. A large
imposing chair, a small table beside
it are almost the only furnishings in
the room; a parsimoniously small fire
burns in the fireplace grate. Taking
off his hat and scarf, he hangs them

by the door. Taking off his frock coat, he exchanges it for an ancient shabby dressinggown. He then goes to the window and opens it. Looking out, he sees nothing but desolate street. He closes the window, locks it, and pulls the heavy tattered curtain across it. Going back to the stove he dishes up a bowl of gruel and, sitting in the big chair, begins to eat. Slowly he becomes aware of a distant sound coming nearer: it is that of heavy chains being dragged up the stairs. He listens more intently, his fear increasing as the sound increases. Finally, the noise becomes almost deafening. Suddenly a great blast of wind bursts open the massive door, the locks still intact. Silence. In the portal stands the gray specter of Scrooge's long dead partner, Jacob Marley. He is dressed in mouldy tattered grave clothes; his arms, legs and torso draped with heavy chains. With great effort he drags them after him into the room. Scrooge, stunned with fear, is unable to move.

MARLEY
(In a hollow commanding voice.) Ebenezer Scrooge. . . . !

SCROOGE
(In utter disbelief.) Jacob. . . !? Jacob Marley? Is it really you?

> The gaze of Marley remains at some point beyond Scrooge. The

> ghost sees and does
> not see.

                    MARLEY

I was he once called Jacob Marley.

> His voice seems to
> come from great
> distances.

                    SCROOGE

Jacob . . . this cannot be. You were
buried seven years ago this very night!
You are dead, Jacob! I myself helped carry
you to the grave.

                    MARLEY

Where even now I lie. This you see of me
is but my tormented spirit. It does not
rest. Doomed to walk until in time my sins
are purged away. My spirit has not known
rest since the day my body sank into that
grave. Seven long and weary years, Ebenezer
Scrooge. . . .

                    SCROOGE

But Jacob . . . friend Jacob . . . why has
this been done to thee?

                    MARLEY

(With a furious shaking of his chains.)
Keep silent, Ebenezer Scrooge!!! I am not
here for idle purpose. My business is grim
and full of desperation. I come from the
farthest reaches of the nether world that
you may yet escape the torments I endure.
I come to spare your soul, wretched man,
if it be not too late, if it be not lost
entirely.

Scene 4   33

SCROOGE

(Subdued with fear, but striving to hold onto his sanity.) Jacob, dear, dear friend . . . do not be offended if I must question if this be true . . . if, in fact, ye do be here.

MARLEY

(With great sadness.) Oh, Ebenezer--I know your mind as I knew my own. I see to the very bottom of your thoughts. (Slowly shaking his head.) You do not believe in me.

SCROOGE

You must admit, Jacob, it is much you ask.

MARLEY

If you do not credit what your eyes attest, say then what you think this sight to be.

SCROOGE

(More the assessing business man now.) I cannot say entirely what this thing--your pardon, Jacob--what you really be. Perhaps the vapors arising from an overwrought imagination . . . perhaps the result of a miserable supper . . . a bit of undigested beef, a crumb of cheese . . . perhaps too much of a heavy pudding. But a ghost, Jacob? That would take more proof than this. . . .

> Marley turns his eyes upward in his head and with slow deliberateness begins a low moan which continues to build in intensity until the sound reaches a

maddening pitch and
volume. Marley's voice
is accompanied by the
shreiks and howls of
other unseen voices
and the rattling of
great lengths of
heavy chain. The din
causes Scrooge to
sink to the floor in
an agony of fear.
When he is almost
prostrate before
Marley, the sound
fades down and out.

SCROOGE

No more! No more, Jacob! Have mercy!
Forgive my doubt! For the sake of old
friendship, <u>no</u> <u>more</u>, <u>I</u> <u>pray</u>!!!

MARLEY

Say then, wretched man, that you <u>believe</u>
<u>in</u> <u>me</u>!

SCROOGE

I do, oh, I do--I do! No more! No more.

MARLEY

And will take to heart all I come to tell
thee?

SCROOGE

I will, Jacob. On my life, I will believe
the smallest word you utter.

MARLEY

Swear, Ebenezer Scrooge!

SCROOGE

Upon my life, I swear.

                    MARLEY
Nay! Not upon thy miserable penurious
existence! Upon thy immortal soul, swear!

                         The word "swear" is
                         echoed by other
                         unseen voices.

                    SCROOGE
Upon my soul, Jacob. I swear! I swear.

                         The manner of the
                         ghost becomes less
                         threatening. He moves
                         closer to Scrooge.

                    MARLEY
Then heed, unhappy man, what I have been
sent so far to say.

                    SCROOGE
(Raising himself to a kneeling position.)
You have but to speak and I'll attend
thee to the last sylable.

                    MARLEY
Hark!

                         He turns slightly
                         away as if hearing
                         some distant summons.

My time with thee is short. Even now I am
called to resume my restless wandering.
Ahhhhhhh . . . how I long to find oblivion!
To rest. To lie quiet in that grave you
put me. (He gives a long mournful sigh.)

SCROOGE

If in any way I can ease your torment, Jacob, let me hear it.

MARLEY

(Coldly and without self-pity.) I am beyond all human aid. No form of prayer will ease my judgment. I come because there still remains a distant hope for thee, not myself.

SCROOGE

But why are you here? In what way have I been amiss?

MARLEY

(A deep and mournful groan.) Ahhhhh . . . blind man. . . .

SCROOGE

(Pressing on in his defense.) I have always been a fair and watchful man of business. Our credit grows yearly--our value in bond and cash, has grown since your death. We are prosperous--men of substance!

> The recounting of the
> financial soundness
> of the firm only
> increases the misery
> of the ghost.

MARLEY

(With frosty pity.) Fool . . . poor fool. The chains you see which bind and weigh me down are of my own forging! They are my hateful greed made manifest in steel. (He shakes his chains in a remorseful fury.) A heavy record of my dealings with my fellow man. Each human feeling I denied in life became another link. Year by year, link by

link, I grew these hateful fetters longer.
Now they are welded to my very soul and I
must bear them many ages yet to come.

                    SCROOGE
(A real concern for another beginning to
take hold.) Is there no hope for thee,
poor ghost?

                    MARLEY
(Wearily.) In time . . . in time. . . .

                              He turns his gaze
                              directly on Scrooge
                              for the first time.

But hark'e, Ebenezer Scrooge: although you
know it not, seven years ago the chains
which you wore even then were as heavy as
these of mine are now.

                    SCROOGE
(Terror stricken.) Ah! Jacob. . . .

                    MARLEY
Oh, foolish man! Could you but see--as I
see--what hideous great chains bind you
at the present time!

                    SCROOGE
No. . . . It is not so! It cannot be so!

                              He looks at his hands
                              in a vain effort to
                              see what Marley sees.
                              He rises from the
                              floor.

Where be they!? I feel them not!

MARLEY
It is so! Like great serpents they coil
around thy immortal soul. Believe it,
wretched man!

SCROOGE
I do . . .. oh, I do.

Scrooge sinks into
his chair. A deep bell
strikes one.

MARLEY
My time with thee has come to an end.

SCROOGE
(Almost inaudible.) . . . Friend Jacob
. . . what can I do to free myself
from that dreadful future you prophesy?

Marley is fast losing
contact with the
mortal world; he
speaks as if intoning
an invocation.

MARLEY
Three spirits will wait upon thee. By
their visions ye may yet come to know the
dreadful shadow in which you stand, and,
knowing that, come to know thyself. Only
when you have peered deep into the darkness
of your own soul might some hope for your
salvation come to light.

Growing weaker, Marley
is pulled by some
force toward the door.

It is there you must begin. Look within
thyself, Ebenezer Scrooge.

Scene 4   39

SCROOGE
(Pleading.) Send no more apparitions to
me, I pray. I will profit by your visit
alone, Jacob. I'll do as you say. . . .

MARLEY
(No longer in the same world as Scrooge.)
Three will come before this night is out.
Until that time, I will give thee sleep,
Ebenezer Scroooooge. . . .

SCROOGE
(Feeling the hypnotic suggestion.) Do not
leave . . . me . . . so.

MARLEY
(Fading.) Sleep . . . sleep, Ebenezer
Scrooge . . . sleep . . . until thy
ghostly visitations . . . sleep . . .
sleep . . . Ebenezer S-C-R-O-O-G-E. . . .

> He vanishes
> completely.

SCROOGE
(Now speaking out of his sleep.) Do . . .
not . . . leave me . . . so . . . do not
leave. . . .

> The light fades
> except for the fire
> in the small grate;
> this glows for a
> moment more and then
> goes out.

ACT II

SCENE 1
Darkness. In the distance a sound of
bells can be heard. But these, unlike
the deep solemn tones of the earlier
bells, are lighter. They are, in fact,
sleigh-bells. They come nearer and
nearer. A cold light builds around
the sleeping Scrooge. With a start,
he wakes to find himself in a shadowed
alleyway near his countinghouse. He
is seated in the same attitude when
last seen, but his familiar
surroundings are gone. Down the
alleyway a young woman with silver-
white hair appears. She wears a crown
of lighted candles and has a wand of
holly in her hand. She approaches
Scrooge with a smile on her lips.

FIRST SPIRIT
Ebenezer Scrooge. . . .

SCROOGE
Where . . . what's this place?

FIRST SPIRIT
Where once you were and are no more.

SCROOGE
Speak plain! What do I here!?

> He is not as
> intimidated by this
> vision as he was of
> Marley. He looks
> around.

Where is my room gone? My chair, my
fireplace, my . . . and who are you!?

FIRST SPIRIT
These things you speak of are but shadows
of the future. They are not yet. This
. . . (she spreads her hands) . . . is the
past. Those things you speak of have yet
to be. They belong to the coming time. I
am the Spirit of Christmas Past. Rise,
Ebenezer Scrooge and follow me to a place
where we may better view times now gone.

SCROOGE
Spirit. . . .

FIRST SPIRIT
Do not tarry. All time is precious. Waste
not this gift of time remembered now
granted thee.

SCROOGE
Nay, Spirit. I am a stranger to
remembrance. My business does not allow
for sentimental journeys to this past land
where you dwell. Leave me be.

FIRST SPIRIT
Come! (More gently.) Come. Trust in me. In
time this I have to show will serve to
bring thee home to thyself.

SCROOGE
But you took me from my home, Spirit.

FIRST SPIRIT
Only from thy house--not thy home.

> They walk. She leads
> him up to a higher
> place.

Scrooge and the Ghost of Christmas Past
Photograph by Butch Nevius

Scene 1   43

                    SCROOGE
Am I to see all that is past, Spirit?

                  FIRST SPIRIT
No, not all. It is only your own past that
concerns us. This I am sent to reveal to
you. I am here to make you welcome to your
memories.

                        She spreads her arms,
                        the edges of the
                        scene expand.

Look. The years fall away. Heed well what
I will now show you, Ebenezer Scrooge.

          SCENE 2
          The office of Scrooge appears, but as
          it was forty years earlier when it
          belonged to Scrooge's first employer,
          Fezziwig.

                    SCROOGE
This is my own countinghouse!

                  FIRST SPIRIT
No. Not yours at this time, Ebenezer
Scrooge. It is not yet become your dark
and cold possession. What you see here now
belongs. . . .

                        As she waves her wand
                        of holly a sprightly
                        rotund little man
                        appears.

. . . to Fezziwig, to whom you are at the
present time apprentice.

SCROOGE
(In wonder.) Fezziwig. . . !

FIRST SPIRIT
Who once you thought the kindest man in all
the world.

SCROOGE
As indeed he was. Old Fezziwig! . . . I
never thought to see him again. Dear kind
old Fezziwig. (His face darkens.) But
Spirit, he . . . he is dead!

FIRST SPIRIT
Not at this time.

SCROOGE
How can this be? He is dead, I say!

FIRST SPIRIT
The past is forever living for those who
choose to remember. He lives because you
remember him alive. He can never die if
you but remember him as he was.

SCROOGE
(Beginning to accept.) Oh, if I could
believe that to be so!

                    Two young men enter
                    with great holly
                    wreaths in their arms.
                    They approach Fezziwig
                    and engage him in a
                    conversation that at
                    the moment cannot be
                    heard.

FIRST SPIRIT
Believe it to be so, Ebenezer Scrooge, for
it is so and there you see it so. But look
again, who stands by his side?

SCROOGE
Dick Wilkins! To be sure--it is he! My old
friend, Dick.

FIRST SPIRIT
Say what else you see. Who is the boy that
stands by his side?

                    Scrooge steps toward
                    the figures.

SCROOGE
My eyes are unaccustomed to this light.
(Comes closer still.) It is . . . myself!
(He turns back.) Oh, cruel spirit! To show
me this!

FIRST SPIRIT
I do not reveal these things to wound, but
with a loving hope: hope that your soul
may warm in these long forgotten sights--
that to see yourself as you were will
return you to what you were. But keep
silent now, Ebenezer Scrooge; we are here
to see and not to judge.

                    The animated
                    conversation between
                    Fezziwig and the boys
                    at this moment becomes
                    audible.

FEZZIWIG
. . . and so, dear lads, clear away! Clear
away, I say! We'd have dancing room.
First, the window shutters. . . .

DICK WILKINS
The shutters are all up, sir, just as you
ordered.

FEZZIWIG
So quick? Good lads, good lads! More light!
More light, chase every shadow hence. More
light, I say!

                              Dick goes off for
                              hanging lamps.

YOUNG EBENEZER
The fiddler's just arrived! He's warming
his hands--can't play, he says, till every
finger is warmed to the proper pitch.

                              Fezziwig laughs with
                              great gusts of
                              wheezing sound.

FEZZIWIG
Just so, just so! And a proper lot of
playing we'll require tonight, boys, so
tell him to warm the digits well and when
they reach the proper temperature, the
ball begins! Tell him so, lad, tell him
so!

                              His manner is
                              infectious. He is the
                              spirit of Christmas
                              personified. He
                              continues to put away
                              ledgers and to clear
                              the area for the
                              dance.

And hang those green wreaths, my fine
fellows! No Christmas proper without great
green wreaths to gladden these sour

work-a-day walls. Hang 'em, I say. Then open wide the doors and call the company in! Time is fleeting. Let us step it out with music and dance!

> He goes to a door and calls out.

Mrs. Fezziwig! My dear Mrs. Fezziwig, I say! Your assistance, my dear, your assistance. The guests are on the door step. Bestir yourself.

> Mrs. Fezziwig enters. An imposing woman with brilliant red hair and a suitable match for Fezziwig. In the meanwhile the boys have undertaken their instructions. The fiddler enters and begins to set up his stand and music on a level which overlooks the cleared floor. As he tunes, the various clerks, friends, and members of Fezziwig's family begin to arrive. Both Fezziwig and Mrs. Fezziwig greet the guests with noisy exhuberance. When the entire company is assembled, Fezziwig steps into the center of the group and claps his hands.

                    FEZZIWIG
Your attention . . . your attention, if
you please! (They quieten.) As is our
custom in this place, each Christmas eve,
we assemble here in love and comradeship.
. . .

                        The group assents
                        with a few "here,
                        here."

. . . And, though mindful of the dear
solemn day we celebrate tomorrow, tonight
we meet for lighter purpose. Not to put
too fine a point on it, we would have you
all in a merry mood!

                        There is cheerful
                        assent from the group.

And what better way to begin than with
music and dance. . . .

                    MRS. FEZZIWIG
And an end to this long preamble, husband.

                        All laugh and cheer
                        more loudly. Fezziwig
                        laughs the loudest at
                        his wife's
                        interruption.

                    FEZZIWIG
Just so, me dear, just so! Maestro, we
trust these (he wiggles his fingers at the
fiddler) are sufficiently warmed to the
task. (The fiddler nods.) And so with no
further spout from me, I pray we all step
to it! What say you Mrs. Fezziwig--are ye
sport!?

Scene 2   49

MRS. FEZZIWIG

And well in season, Mr. Fezziwig, well in season! Strike up fiddler!

> The company explodes into noise and laughter. The fiddler begins the music and a lively dance ensues. Scrooge views the activity with fond attention. At the end of the dance, the two young men carry on trays of mugs and a large bowl of punch. Fezziwig takes charge of the dispensing of the drink assisted by Mrs. Fezziwig and the apprentices.

FEZZIWIG

Refreshment for all! My special punch. This is work that raises a thirst. Pass around, lads! Pass around. No second cup without a first.

> When all have a cup, he pounds on some solid surface with his own to gain the attention of the company.

Kind ladies--gallant gentlemen. I'd have your attention for the briefest of moments.

> His wife cocks a warning eye at him.

                    MRS. FEZZIWIG
Husband?

                    FEZZIWIG
Your indulgence, my dear. But a necessary
duty.

                    MRS. FEZZIWIG
Well, no windy words. Be brief.

                         Fezziwig nods that he
                         will. He then steps
                         to the center of the
                         floor. The company
                         quietens.

                    FEZZIWIG
My friends, tonight is a special night--
because it is Christmas eve? Yes, that
makes it special to us all, each and every
one. A very special one for the house of
Fezziwig. But this night is more particular
yet.

                         He crosses to Young
                         Ebenezer and fondly
                         puts his arm around
                         his shoulder.

For the truth of the matter is, our own
dear good lad, Ebenezer, ends this very
day his 'prenticeship to the firm of
Fezziwig!

                         There is good-natured
                         applause and cheering
                         for the accomplishment.

He has served us well. And, had I my
selfish whim, I'd keep him on for many a
term more. Still, the time is come he must

Scene 2   51

make his own way in the world. What say we
send him into his future life with all
good wishes and a lusty cheer!? Hip-hip.
. . .

                    ALL
Hooray!

                    FEZZIWIG
Hip-hip. . . .

                    ALL
Hooray!!

                    FEZZIWIG
Hip-hip. . . .

                    ALL
HOORAY!!!

                              A tumultuous applause
                              follows. Old Scrooge
                              is as pleased with
                              this memory as Young
                              Scrooge is to be
                              living it.

                    FEZZIWIG
And now I think it most appropriate for a
chorus of a well-suited song. Mrs.
Fezziwig, will ye do us the honor?

                    MRS. FEZZIWIG
(In her hearty contralto.)
Should auld acquaintance be forgot
And never brought to mind.
Should auld acquaintance be forgot
And days of auld lang syne.

ALL

For auld lang syne, my dear,
For auld lang syne.
We'll take of cup of kindness yet,
For auld lang syne.

> She clutches Young
> Ebenezer to her ample
> breast, her eyes
> flowing tears.
> Fezziwig shakes him by
> the hand as do several
> others. Young Ebenezer
> is moved almost to
> tears as is Old
> Scrooge.

YOUNG EBENEZER

Say but the word, sir, I'll stay a dozen
terms more!

FEZZIWIG

(Laughing.) I believe you would, young
rascal! Just for these parties, I warrant
ye! Just for the parties.

YOUNG EBENEZER

Indeed, sir. But for more, believe me, sir,
for more.

MRS. FEZZIWIG

And for my cooking as well, Mr. Fezziwig.
That figures too, sir.

FEZZIWIG

And now a good evening to you all and the
merriest of Christmas seasons.

ALL

A very merry Christmas to you, Mr.
Fezziwig.

                              The fiddler begins a
                              slower more stately
                              tune, the scene
                              begins to take on the
                              quality of a fading
                              dream. The guests
                              take their leave.
                              Fezziwig, and Mrs.
                              Fezziwig, young
                              Ebenezer between
                              them, are the last to
                              go. Old Scrooge comes
                              forward into the
                              empty room now full
                              of shadows.

                    SCROOGE
They were kind to me, Spirit. All were
kind in the house of Fezziwig.

                    FIRST SPIRIT
You were loved--and you were loving.

                    SCROOGE
Is that really as I was?

                    FIRST SPIRIT
It was even so, Ebenezer Scrooge.

                    SCROOGE
(Turns away.) How can these things long
dead be living now?

                    FIRST SPIRIT
As you believe them to be so, so they are.
Nor do I reveal anything that does not lie
within you still.

                    SCROOGE
I have forgotten so much . . . so much.

54   Act II

                    FIRST SPIRIT
(Quietly stating a simple truth.) And now
you have remembered.

                              The scene is growing
                              dimmer; Scrooge's
                              gaze becomes
                              thoughtful.

                    SCROOGE
Spirit. . . ?

                              Scrooge moves out of
                              the room.

                    FIRST SPIRIT
What more would you have, Ebenezer Scrooge?

                    SCROOGE
(Shaking his head.) Nothing . . . nothing.

                              He stops by the place
                              where Bob Cratchit's
                              desk would stand.

But I should like to be able to say a word
to my own clerk, Bob Cratchit.

                    FIRST SPIRIT
Such an opportunity will in due course be
granted thee.

                    SCROOGE
(Suddenly.) Spirit! Remove me from this
place.

                    FIRST SPIRIT
I have only shown you that which was.

SCROOGE

Remove me, I say! I cannot bear it! I cannot bear it more. Haunt me no more. Leave me. Take me back to the time you found me. Take me back to where I have learned to live.

FIRST SPIRIT

And would you forget again what you have found again tonight?

SCROOGE

Yes! . . . Spirit, (torn between two worlds). . . . No. These memories burn.

FIRST SPIRIT

A healing fire. A warming fire.

SCROOGE

(Pleading.) Mercy. As you have the power to take me hence from here, Spirit, use it!

FIRST SPIRIT

(Smiles.) As you wish, Ebenezer Scrooge, so it will be.

> The First Spirit waves the branch of holly. Scrooge and the First Spirit are left alone in a small circle of cold light.

My time is almost gone, Ebenezer Scrooge. The river of time flows on. The present crowds upon us.

SCROOGE

Spirit. . . . What is to come? Must I see more? Must I endure more than this?

FIRST SPIRIT
(Becoming more detached.) You will
presently be visited by my brother spirit.
What he has to show, he must himself
reveal.

>The wind is again
>rising. The First
>Spirit begins to
>leave the restricted
>circle of light.

I am over-stayed my time. Ponder well in
days to come this that has been shown you.
I pray you, take back into your heart
these long forgotten memories relived
again tonight. Remember and be healed.

SCROOGE
(Suddenly reconsidering his desire to
leave.) Spirit! One moment more in this
time.

FIRST SPIRIT
(Unheeding of Scrooge's request.) The past
fades and I with it. Ponder well, Ebenezer
Scrooge what I have shown you. Remember
that which was. . . .

>And the First Spirit
>has vanished. Scrooge
>is alone. The wind
>rises to a higher
>pitch. He draws his
>dressinggown tighter
>about him. His fear
>returns.

SCROOGE
(Plaintively.) Spirit. . . !?

                    FIRST SPIRIT
(Her voice now mixed with the wind.)
Remember. . . . Remember. . . .
Ebenezer Scrooge. . . .

                              Echos of his call
                              resound throughout
                              the empty dark space.
                              Again he hears his
                              name in the wind
                              repeated again and
                              again.

                    SCROOGE
Spirit!!?

        SCENE 3
        The deep bell strikes two. As the
        reverberation subsides, a deep
        roaring laughter emerges from the
        darkness. Distant at first, it
        rapidly comes closer. Scrooge peers
        about him but sees nothing. Suddenly,
        a torch appears in the gloom, then a
        second, then a third. Dark-robed
        figures can just be discerned. They
        sing a Christmas canticle made of
        many different carols. The sound is
        both joyous and unsettling. It has a
        certain wildness to it which causes
        Scrooge to feel a fearful unease.
        [Directions following CANTICLE are
        simultaneously performed with music.]

THE CANTICLE OF CHRISTMAS PRESENT*

WOMEN

La-La-La-La, La-La-La-La,
La-La-La-La, La-La-La-La,
La-La-La-La, La-La-La-La,
La-La-La-La, La-La-La-La,
La-La-La-La, La-La-La-La,
La-La-La-La, La-La-La-La,

MEN

Ebenezer. . . .
Ebenezer. . . .
God rest you
Merry gentlemen
Let nothing you
　　　　dismay.
　　　　. . .

BOTH

Dame get up and bake your pies,
Bake your Pies. Bake your pies.
Dame get up and bake your pies
On Christmas day in the. . . .

WOMEN

Good King Wenceslas looked
　　　　out
On the Feast of Stephen

When the snow lay round
　　　　about,
Deep and crisp and even.
Dame what makes your ducks
　　　　to die.

MEN

. . . morning

La-La-La-La-
　　　　La-La.

BOTH

Ducks to die, ducks to die.
Dame what makes your ducks to die. . . .

*Words and music appear at the end of this
script as Appendix A.

Scene 3　　　　　　　　　　　　　　　　59

WOMEN	MEN
On Christmas day in the morning.	Dame what makes your ducks to die On Christmas day in. .

BOTH
Their wings are cut, they cannot fly.
Their wings are cut, they cannot fly.
Their wings are cut, they cannot fly.
On Christmas day in the. . . .
EBENEZER SCROOGE!!!

During the music figures holding small lanterns join the torches until a great mass of flickering fire has formed. The single laughter has also been joined by that of the figures holding the lights. The lights weave and bob; then, out of the center a large bearded figure appears. He is dressed in a massive burgundy velvet robe trimmed in ermine. He is both regal and common at the same time. While jovial, a certain hard practicality lurks beneath his surface manner. Scrooge at once feels he knows the mind of the man who stands before him;

at the same time knows that this spirit will reveal to him things he would, if he could, avoid. As he comes closer to where Scrooge stands, it can be seen that great festoons of fruits and food stuffs hang from his shoulders, his long dark hair encircled with grapes and vine leaves. He is like some gigantic overladen banquet table made human. Trailing him and at his side are several young pages carrying large trays heaped with all manner of holiday food and drink. They, like the lights, move in slow swirling patterns around the figure. Scrooge becomes increasingly uncomfortable as the phantasmagorical vision of Christmas feasting threatens to engulf him. At the wave of his hands, the great figure brings the movement of the lights and trays to a rest.

Spirit of Christmas Present
Photograph by Butch Nevius

SECOND SPIRIT

(Expansively.) I am the Spirit of Christmas Present! Look upon me! You have never seen the like of me before!

SCROOGE

Indeed, Spirit, I have not.

SECOND SPIRIT

That because thou art a miser! (He gives the word its most stinging value.) And yet, petty man, I am sent for thy good and instruction. To that end, Ebenezer Scrooge . . . (again a biting tone to the name) I invite thee to partake of these my ample offerings: eat and drink your fill!

>He gestures broadly
>again and the trays
>of food are brought
>at various levels
>within the reach of
>Scrooge. He cringes
>as if they were
>poisonous.

SCROOGE

Nay, Spirit. I have suffered much in the past from too rich foods. Plainer fare far is more to my liking, better suited to my needs.

SECOND SPIRIT

(Sneeringly.) A miserly sentiment--a miserable philosophy. Pleasures of the grand table are much a part of the Christmas season. Once more, I bid thee take from us samplings of our feast!

>At his signal, the
>movement of the lights

> begin and the boys
> with the trays move
> more inticingly
> around Scrooge. There
> is more than a touch
> of the pagan to this
> display; Scrooge is
> horrified by the
> excessive quality of
> the vision.

SCROOGE

Have mercy, Spirit! I have told thee
plainly--this feasting is not in my nature.
Call off these demons of rich meat and
drink! Call them off! I will have none of
it! Have mercy, Spirit!!!

> The Second Spirit
> allows Scrooge to be
> tormented a short
> while longer but then,
> with a broad gesture,
> he brings the movement
> to rest.

I am obliged to you, Spirit. I am not a
well man, my stomach is delicate.

SECOND SPIRIT

A miser, Scrooge, in plain and simple
truth--a miser. Well, since you would have
your Christmas feast less rich, I'll take
thee to a place where frugal holidays are
all that can be observed, a place where my
delights are all but unknown.

> At the wave of his
> hand the figures fade
> away.

A place where love and kindness must serve to fill out a meager pudding. (As he begins to leave, the warm light changes to cold.) Touch my robe, Ebenezer Scrooge.

                    SCROOGE
(Holding back.) If, perhaps. . . .

                    SECOND SPIRIT
(Imperiously.) Touch my robe!!! Follow where I lead!

        SCENE 4
        Scrooge decides this is the wisest course to follow and does as he is commanded. As he places his hand on the arm of the Second Spirit, the wind rises quickly and swift-moving patterns cross over the two. As the wind dies down, peals of childish laughter can be heard in the darkness. Then, the light of a parlor fireplace begins to glow. As the light builds, the home of Bob Cratchit is revealed. A young girl and a slightly older boy are playfully setting a small table for evening tea. They are interrupted by the good-natured scolding of Mrs. Cratchit, who enters from the kitchen with a large bowl in her arms and a wooden spoon in her hand.

                    MRS. CRATCHIT
Children! What a noise! Peter. . . . Belinda!

                    PETER
Yes mother?

MRS. CRATCHIT
The noise, my dears--the noise! I have cakes in the oven. Do ye want them falling?

BELINDA
(With real concern.) Oh, no, mother!

MRS. CRATCHIT
Then pray, (she lowers her voice to a whisper) a--lit--tle--more--quiet.

PETER
We're very sorry, mother.

MRS. CRATCHIT
(Smiles.) And now, my treasures, you must see the table properly set. I have a thousand things left to do. Now, have I your promise?

BOTH
Yes, mother.

MRS. CRATCHIT
And where might be your father and Tim?

PETER
They stayed at the church for a little longer.

MRS. CRATCHIT
Did Tim tire himself out?

BELINDA
Oh, no, mama. He said the lights were so pretty this year that the longer he looked at them the longer he would remember and if he looked long enough he could make them last until next year.

                    MRS. CRATCHIT
Well . . . he so loves bright things. But
it is getting colder. I wish they would
come home.

                    PETER
Mother. . . .

                    MRS. CRATCHIT
Yes, my dear?

                    PETER
Is Tim getting better?

                    MRS. CRATCHIT
(Pause.) We are all going to be just fine.
Now, mend the fire so that they can warm
themselves when they come out of the cold
night air. (Leaving.) And when you finish
here--this bowl will need a good licking
out in the kitchen.

                    BELINDA
Have we a great plum pudding this year?

                    MRS. CRATCHIT
So big it will take the both of you to
carry it to table.

                              This excites both
                              children to a frenzy
                              of last minute
                              preparations. Mrs.
                              Cratchit returns to
                              the kitchen. A moment
                              later the front door
                              slams.

BELINDA
It's papa! Get some coals for the fire.
He'll be wanting to make the hot punch
soon.

TINY TIM (Offstage)
Don't drop me papa!

BOB CRATCHIT (Offstage)
No fear, my boy. (Coming into the room,
Tiny Tim on his back.) All right, this is
as far as you go.

> He puts Tiny Tim down
> and then begins to
> sport with all the
> children. The noise
> increases to a high
> level. Mrs. Cratchit
> returns with a lighted
> candle which she
> places on the mantel
> of the fireplace.

MRS. CRATCHIT
I might have known, Bob Cratchit, you
would be the biggest child of all!

BOB CRATCHIT
And hope to remain so, my dear, for the
rest of my years!

MRS. CRATCHIT
No fear of that husband. No fear of that.

> The children have
> settled down in a
> corner playing some
> quiet game.

BOB CRATCHIT

(Going to the fire.) How good it is, wife, to come out of the cold. A bitter night. Scarce a soul left on the streets. (Stirs the fire with a poker.) This fire's a proper blessing. Did you make it, Peter?

PETER

(Proudly.) Yes, sir. I did.

BELINDA

I helped!

PETER

But I got the blaze going!

BELINDA

And who carried the starting wood?

BOB CRATCHIT

(Laughing.) Children! Children! We are all necessary for the good of each--and each does his part for the good of all. That's a lesson you must never forget, eh, Peter? Belinda?

BOTH

(Slightly chastened.) Yes, papa.

TINY TIM

(Chiming in from the corner.) I know that too, papa.

BOB CRATCHIT

(Very fondly.) I know you do, Tim. (A slight pause.) And now, mother--are your kitchen chores well in hand?

MRS. CRATCHIT

All's on husband. Just the watching's left to do.

Scene 4

BOB CRATCHIT
Good--because I have here. . . .

> He begins to remove
> from his pockets the
> wrapped bottles for
> the making of the
> special punch they
> always have on
> Christmas eve.

all ingredients necessary for our most
glorious concoction! Our annual Christmas
punch.

> Mrs. Cratchit takes
> them from him and
> looks at the wrapping.

MRS. CRATCHIT
Oh, husband--a dear price!

BOB CRATCHIT
(With his finger on her lips.) Not a word
this night of expense, dear lady. A
special night demands a special treat . . .
and the expense be hanged! Let that be the
watchword for the night: The expense be
hanged!!

MRS. CRATCHIT
I'll allow ye to be right this one night,
Mr. Cratchit. But nonetheless. . . .

BOB CRATCHIT
But, nothing.

> He tweaks her ear and
> kisses her on the
> cheek.

MRS. CRATCHIT
Husband! The children!

BOB CRATCHIT
Speaking of children--and where's our
eldest daughter? It's well past the time
she promised.

TINY TIM
(At the window.) No need to worry, papa.
She's just now turned into our street.

BOB CRATCHIT
(Bustling.) Not a moment to lose, children!
Peter, make sure the poker is sizzling hot
to plunge into the punch. It must be red
hot if the flavors are to blend properly.

PETER
May I do it this year, father?

BOB CRATCHIT
(A moment's consideration.) And why not? I
believe you're of an age to undertake such
an obligation. And so you will, my boy!
But have we cups enough? Belinda, my dear,
fetch from the pantry the cinnamon sticks.

TINY TIM
(Excited.) She's almost on the doorstep!

MRS. CRATCHIT
Poor thing, must be perished with the cold.

BOB CRATCHIT
(Calling after Belinda.) And don't forget
the cloves, my dear. (To his wife.) How I
have looked forward to this hot Christmas
punch, wife. I am almost thankful we have

it but once a year--the waiting is as good
as the drink itself.

MRS. CRATCHIT
For my part, I'm sure I'd have it once a
week, could our purse stand the traffic.

> The front door slams.
> Tiny Tim is up in a
> flash.

TINY TIM
She's here! She's here! Martha's here!

> Martha enters carrying
> a few small packages
> with her.

MRS. CRATCHIT
My dear girl. (Hugs her.) Here, give me
your things.

> Mrs. Cratchit helps
> with her shawl and
> hat.

MARTHA
I'm sorry mother . . . father . . . (She
hugs him and kisses him on the cheek.) At
the last minute we had three more hats
apiece to finish and the shop had to be
set to order.

MRS. CRATCHIT
Well, at last you're here--and that is all
that matters. We are so pleased to see you
daughter.

BOB CRATCHIT
Indeed, we are. Best wishes of the season
to you, my child.

MRS. CRATCHIT

Sit before the fire, my dear, and have a good warm, Lord bless ye!

MARTHA

First, let me give you these. . . .

> She begins to distribute the small packages to the children and to her parents. Belinda returns with the spices. She runs to her sister and hugs her.

BELINDA

Martha! I didn't hear you come in, sister.

TINY TIM

She certainly made enough noise.

> They all laugh.

MARTHA

They aren't much, but. . . .

BOB CRATCHIT

Not much!? Put 'em in a scale with the Queen's own crown and I'll wager which would come up the lighter. Not these gifts my dear.

MARTHA

(Pleased at the simple gratitude of her family.) I hope you like them.

> They all assure her they do. She has saved the biggest

> package for last. This
> goes to Tiny Tim who
> is, of course, the
> darling of the family.
> She kneels down
> beside him as she
> gives him his gift.

And this for you, Tim.

                    TINY TIM
(His eyes wide with excitement.) Thank you
very much, Martha. (He kisses her cheek.)
May I open it now?

                    MARTHA
Of course! I wouldn't for the world have
you wait a moment longer.

> The wrappings are
> quickly removed. A
> large wooden soldier
> in bright paint
> emerges.

                    TINY TIM
Oh . . . sister! He's the finest soldier
I've ever seen! Look, everyone!

> In his excitement, he
> forgets to use his
> crutch and almost
> falls. Martha catches
> him in time. All have
> instinctively tensed
> to his aid, however.
> He recovers quickly,
> the soldier still
> firmly in his hands.

Someday I'd be just such a soldier! What a
fine big black moustache he has.

                    PETER
It'll be a month or two, Tim, before you'll
sport one as big.

                    They all laugh.

                    BOB CRATCHIT
(The slightest hint of sadness in his
voice.) And a right good soldier you will
make, my boy. No doubt a general some day
to boot, eh, Tim?

                    TINY TIM
No . . . just a soldier.

                    BOB CRATCHIT
But now--the punch! Is the poker hot enough,
Peter?

                    PETER
Yes, sir. Hot and ready!

                    BOB CRATCHIT
News worth hearing! (Picks up the pitcher.)
Now to your task, boy! Mull us up a pitcher
of Bob Cratchit's Special Christmas Brew!

                    Peter takes the poker,
                    plunges it into the
                    liquid. A great
                    sizzling and the punch
                    is done.

Come! Your cups! Your cups! Piping hot! It
must be drunk piping hot! Not a moment to
spare. Your cups!

MRS. CRATCHIT

You mustn't overheat yourself more than
the punch.

> But Bob Cratchit
> plainly enjoys the
> excitement he creates
> with this annual
> ritual. He fills up
> the various glasses
> and oddly assorted
> cups. Last of all he
> fills his own small
> glass. There is none
> left in the pitcher
> and his own portion
> is small.

Here, Bob! You've left precious little for
yourself. Here, take some of mine.

> He holds up one finger
> to stop his wife from
> giving him any of hers

BOB CRATCHIT

(Kindly but firmly.) Exactly the amount I
planned, mother. To the drop. (She knows
not to insist.) And now: I propose a very
merry Christmas to us all, my dears. And
let us also drink the health and well
being of Mr. Scrooge, the Founder of the
Feast we have on Christmas day.

MRS. CRATCHIT

The Founder of the Feast, indeed! I wish I
had him here. I'd give him a piece of my
mind to feast upon, and I hope he'd have a
good appetite for it.

BOB CRATCHIT
My dear, the children! Remember the day.

MRS. CRATCHIT
It should be Christmas eve, I'm sure, on
which one drinks the health of such an
odious, stingy, hard, unfeeling man as Mr.
Scrooge. You know he is, Bob! Nobody knows
it better than you do!

BOB CRATCHIT
My dear--Christmas eve. Let our hearts be
filled with joy this night. We have so
much to be thankful for. And most of all,
we have the dear company of each other.

MRS. CRATCHIT
(Softening.) Well--I'll drink his health
for your sake, Bob Cratchit, and the
day's--not for his. So, long life to him!
And a merry Christmas and a happy New Year!
He'll be very merry and very happy, I have
no doubt.

BOB CRATCHIT
So then, God bless us all in the future as
he has this night.

ALL
God bless us all.

MRS. CRATCHIT
(Softening even more.) And even Mr. Scrooge.

ALL
(Merrily.) And even Mr. Scrooge.

TINY TIM
(Brightly.) God bless us--_every_ _one_!

BOB CRATCHIT
(Smiling.) Quite so, my dear--God bless
us--every one.

> They drink. A moment
> of silence while they
> savor this holiday
> treat and the company
> of each other. The
> light dims to a lower
> level but the scene
> remains.

SECOND SPIRIT
This sight should please your frugal soul,
Scrooge. Nothing in excess here--nothing
wasted. And some might say not quite
enough.

SCROOGE
I would, Spirit, that Bob Cratchit had a
bit more for his own portion.

SECOND SPIRIT
That is hardly possible, considering the
wage he makes--or should I say "robs" from
your pocket every three hundred and sixty
fifth day?

SCROOGE
(Genuinely moved by the scene just
witnessed.) Do not taunt me thus, Spirit.
The error of my past ways crowds too fast
upon me. To change is often painful. To
change takes time.

SECOND SPIRIT
Time? And how much of that most precious
gift, do you think, is left to you,
Scrooge?!

SCROOGE
(Looks back at the Cratchit household.)
Enough, I hope. Indeed, at this moment, it
is my fondest hope. . . . To have a little
time more.

SECOND SPIRIT
To collect more interest on the cold store
of gold you possess?

SCROOGE
No, Spirit. I would use my time for better
purpose.

SECOND SPIRIT
(A low deep understanding laugh.) So? But
look once more before this vision fades.

> As the Spirit and
> Scrooge conversed, the
> children slowly left
> the room for bed. Bob
> Cratchit and his wife
> have taken their place
> before the dying fire
> and are quietly
> enjoying a peaceful
> moment.

MRS. CRATCHIT
And how did little Tim behave in church
tonight?

BOB CRATCHIT
As good as gold, my dear, and better. But
somehow he gets thoughtful sitting by
himself so much. . . . And he thinks the
strangest things you ever heard. He told
me, coming home, that he hoped . . .
(trying to remember the exact words) . . .
he hoped all the people saw him in church.

MRS. CRATCHIT
(Quietly.) How strange. What do ye think
prompted him to that, husband?

BOB CRATCHIT
(Still quoting.) Because he was a cripple
. . . and it might be pleasant to them, he
said, to remember upon Christmas day, who
made lame beggars walk and blind men see.

> They both are moved
> to silence by this
> and sit looking into
> the low fire.

SCROOGE
(Also greatly moved.) Oh, Spirit. . . .

> But the Second Spirit
> signals him to keep
> silent.

MRS. CRATCHIT
Well, my dear, if our love can make him
sound and strong, he'll be the greatest
soldier England ever had.

> Her husband rises and
> goes to her side. In
> the distance a band
> of carolers are heard
> approaching. Bob
> Cratchit goes to the
> mantle, takes down
> the candle, and places
> it in the window. The
> singers outside are
> singing "Silent Night.

Tiny Tim
Photograph by Butch Nevius

When the song is
finished, Bob Cratchit
gently helps his wife
up and they leave. The
scene fades. The low
wind returns. Scrooge
and the Second Spirit
are once again in the
dark void.

SCROOGE

Spirit, perhaps I could. . . .

SECOND SPIRIT

Our time grows short, Ebenezer Scrooge.
Come away from this place. Other sights
await you.

SCROOGE

Will he die, Spirit?

SECOND SPIRIT

Who?

SCROOGE

Their smallest son--Tiny Tim.

SECOND SPIRIT

(Nonchalantly.) And what concern could
that possibly be to you? After all, if he
is to die, best he should do it soon and
decrease the surplus population.

SCROOGE

(Greatly stung by his own words turned on
him.) No . . . no! Spirit--I am not the
man who spoke those words.

SECOND SPIRIT

What hypocrisy is this!? They are your
very words! Your words!

SCROOGE

I am as different from he as this night is
from that day! Believe it, Spirit! I am
not that man!

SECOND SPIRIT

Words once spoke do not so easily die,
Scrooge. Would you have me believe one
night's visions could melt such a hardened
heart?

SCROOGE

(Plaintively but not abjectly.) I would!
Yes, I would--and would welcome opportunity
to prove it too. And prove it I would,
Spirit!

> The Second Spirit does
> not answer. The great
> bell strikes three
> times.

SECOND SPIRIT

As to that I cannot know. This you would
have lies within the domain of my brother
spirit. As for me, I am now called to
close my visitation with you. The longest
night will have an end, but one more
spirit yet must follow in my steps. Prepare
for him, Ebenezer Scrooge. He brings no
feasting, no fire, and no fond memories as
we who came before. His gifts may prove
more frugal yet. Look for him when I am
gone. . . .

> The Second Spirit
> begins to fade.

Look for him. . . .

And Scrooge is left
again in very little
light.

SCROOGE

Spirit! Wait. Tell me! When may I expect
this last vision? Speak!

SCENE 5
The Third Spirit steps out from the
shadows. He wears a heavy black robe,
his face hidden beneath the hood. His
voice is stern; his manner
unyieldingly direct.

THIRD SPIRIT

I am already with you, Ebenezer Scrooge.

SCROOGE

(Startled.) I did not hear your coming,
Spirit. Nor did I think to know your
presence so soon.

THIRD SPIRIT

I am that which appears before expectation.
Yet ere I am sought, I am already here. I
am the Spirit of Christmas Yet to Come.

SCROOGE

(To himself.) Too soon . . . too soon. . . .

THIRD SPIRIT

Come, Scrooge! My business, like yours,
will not wait upon the leisure of that
"mad world of fools" you so despise.

SCROOGE

(Wearily.) A moment, Spirit. I am in need
of rest. I have been far this night.

                    THIRD SPIRIT
And farther still must go before this
night is done. Come!

                    SCROOGE
But Spirit. . . .

                    THIRD SPIRIT
(His voice becomes more steely.) Time and
kindness you have denied in full measure
to mankind, Scrooge. In the account of
human feeling you are all but bankrupt.
Even now, your debts stand overdue and
demand full payment. Come! Or forever stay
in this dark night.

                              Scrooge stands fixed
                              at this harsh
                              indictment. The Third
                              Spirit extends his
                              hand to Scrooge. With
                              horror, Scrooge sees
                              that it has no flesh
                              on it.

                    SCROOGE
I pray you, set me free from these wild
and horrible dreams!

                              He steps forward and
                              scans the dark skies.

Jacob!? Jacob!? If you hear, take these
visions from me! (To the Third Spirit.) I
cannot go on.

                              He sinks to his knees,
                              the Third Spirit
                              standing over him.

THIRD SPIRIT
Then I will bring the scene to you. Look
where I would have you see.

SCENE 6
A tenament section of London near the
river. An old crone approaches a
doorway in a shadowy alleyway. She
carries a large loosely tied bundle.
Looking about to ensure she is not
seen, she knocks at the door. No
answer. She knocks again. After a
moment the door opens slightly; a low
raspy voice issues from the crack.

VOICE
What's it ye want!?

OLD CRONE
(Secretly.) I got something here.

VOICE
Eh!?

OLD CRONE
(A louder whisper.) I got something here!
Something ye might take a fancy to.

VOICE
Be off!

OLD CRONE
(Quickly.) Quality it is--and cheap. I'll
go cheap.

The door opens a
little wider. A
hideous bent figure
comes into view.

                    OLD MAN
Well? What's the business?

                    OLD CRONE
(Looking around before opening the end of
the bundle she carries.) These.

                    OLD MAN
Bed linens?! Curtains?

                    OLD CRONE
Quality.

                    OLD MAN
(Feeling the material.) Old--very old.

                    OLD CRONE
(Quickly.) But quality! Very finely made.
Still good.

                    OLD MAN
Ay . . . but old. (He looks more
searchingly at her.) Seed you before, I
have. You work hereabouts?

                    OLD CRONE
Housekeeper.

                    OLD MAN
These be missed?

                    OLD CRONE
(A hacking laugh.) Not by him who had 'em.

                    OLD MAN
(Looking deep into her face.) You be . . .
you be old Scrooge's house drudge?

                    OLD CRONE
No more. (Shakes head.) No more.

                         OLD MAN
Eh?

                        OLD CRONE
Cold as a stone he be. No longer need for
these bed covers.

                         OLD MAN
Dead!? Old Scrooge be dead then?

                        OLD CRONE
He be as stiff and hard as that heart of
his always was. (A low mirthless laugh.)
So . . . what will ye gi' for these?
Quality, I say, and you see it.

                         OLD MAN
Dead, eh? (Then to business. He assesses
the loot.) Two shilling--six pence . . .
no more.

                        OLD CRONE
Ahhhhh! Ye be robbin' me!

                         OLD MAN
Call not the kettle black! Two shilling--
six pence! Na' a penny more!

                        OLD CRONE
(Hesitates, then nods.) So be, so be.

                         OLD MAN
(Taking out purse.) It's me who comes out
short on this. Old goods--hard to sell.
(Pays her the coins.) Old. . . . Near worn
out.

                        OLD CRONE
Thieving old cheat! As bad as him who lyed
in these sheets! (Bites coin.)

OLD MAN

Be off, hag!

> The old crone makes
> an evil-eye gesture
> at him and slinks
> back into the shadows.
> The old man disappears
> behind the closed
> door. The scene fades.

SCROOGE

(Coming forward.) Before I be cold,
Spirit . . . My possessions stolen and
sold?

THIRD SPIRIT

You have no need of earthly warmth,
Scrooge. You have yourself many times
foreclosed on the property of the dead
with businesslike haste. A matter of
survival only for those left in this world.

SCROOGE

So soon . . . so soon. . . .

THIRD SPIRIT

Look again.

> SCENE 7
> The Third Spirit moves the skeletal
> finger to indicate another spot some
> distance from where they stand. As
> Scrooge watches, a small area in
> front of his own office is revealed.
> It is a cold winter morning.

THIRD SPIRIT

Do you know this place?

SCROOGE
(Puzzled.) How should I not know this
place? I know it as well as the back of my
own hand: it is before my own countinghouse.
My own office.

THIRD SPIRIT
Say--what more do you see?

SCROOGE
What more is there to see? I have walked
here a thousand times.

THIRD SPIRIT
And is all as it was?

SCROOGE
(Searching for the meaning behind this
insistent questioning.) All seems . . .
No! The sign--my sign! Is gone!! (The Old
Scrooge reappears.) What thieves and
vandals have done this thing? To remove a
man's own property!!! I'll have the law!
Who has done this!?

THIRD SPIRIT
(Coldly quiet.) I have done this, Ebenezer
Scrooge. It was this hand that took your
name away.

SCROOGE
(Pitifully confused.) But why? For what
cause have you done this?

THIRD SPIRIT
That have I come to show in full. Stand
aside; let the future pass.

                He points toward a
                side street. Two young

                    businessmen enter in
                    high spirits.

                    FIRST MAN
Ha, ha, ha . . . is it even so?

                    SECOND MAN
I swear it!

                    FIRST MAN
The word was, he was too obstinate to die.

                    SECOND MAN
That's true enough.

                    FIRST MAN
I've even heard that when he did arrive at
the gates of Heaven, St. Peter refused
entry, whereupon arriving at the other
place, he would not be let in because the
Devil <u>couldn't</u> <u>stand</u> <u>the</u> <u>competition</u>!

                    The Second Man roars
                    with laughter. The
                    First Man quickly
                    goes on.

So it was decided to let him stay eternally
on earth--that it was mutually agreed
between Heaven and Hell that such a place,
as this world be, deserved no better in
the first place.

                    The Second Man wipes
                    the tears of laughter
                    from his eyes.

                    SECOND MAN
Well--all jesting aside . . . (looking up
at where Scrooge's sign used to hang)
. . . it will not be the same old street.

Something's gone, that's for sure. Miserly old reprobate that he was.

                    FIRST MAN
But is it something that will be missed? That's the question.

                    SECOND MAN
(Shrugs.) Hard to say . . . hard to say.

                         Scrooge, who has been
                         attending this
                         conversation with
                         ever-mounting horror
                         turns to the Third
                         Spirit.

                    SCROOGE
Spirit. . !?

                         The Third Spirit
                         silences him with a
                         gesture.

                    THIRD SPIRIT
There is more, Ebenezer Scrooge, more. Attend. . . .

                         He points in another
                         direction; Bob
                         Cratchit appears. He
                         no longer has the
                         jaunty gait or his
                         ever-present air of
                         optimism about him.

                    SECOND MAN
Here's the old scoundrel's former clerk, Bob Cratchit.

FIRST MAN
I know him, a very good man.

SECOND MAN
Good day, Mr. Cratchit.

FIRST MAN
Good day.

CRATCHIT
(Distractedly.) Sir? (Then, recognizing the
two men.) Oh, I beg your pardon. I'm afraid
I was. . . .

FIRST MAN
(Aware that he is disturbed.) Yes, well
. . . we have not seen you of late, Mr.
Cratchit.

CRATCHIT
(Shakes his head.) No . . . I do not often
walk this way since the closing of the
firm.

> Scrooge catches his
> breath; he wants
> desperately to come
> forward and assure
> all present that the
> firm of Scrooge and
> Marley still exists.

SECOND MAN
We should like to impart to you our sincere
condolences on the passing of your employer,
Ebenezer Scrooge.

SCROOGE
Ahhh. . . .

>He steps toward the
>three attempting to
>break the impossible
>barrier of time.

I am alive! Bob Cratchit . . . I am not
dead! Hear me!

>CRATCHIT

Thank you, sir.

>SCROOGE

I'm <u>alive</u>!

>FIRST MAN

And also our heartfelt grief to hear of
the death of your youngest son. His name
was. . . .

>CRATCHIT

Tim. We called him . . . Tiny Tim. (A
slight pause.) Thank you sir, my humble
thanks to both. My wife and family will
appreciate the kindness of those wishes.

>SECOND MAN

We saw the two of you often. He seemed a
brave little lad.

>Bob Cratchit nods.

>FIRST MAN

Will your new work keep you in this street,
do you think?

>CRATCHIT

(Without great enthusiasm.) Yes. Yes, I
believe it will for a time at least. Mr.
Scrooge's nephew has taken a suite of
offices down the street. He has been kind

enough to take me on. I'm just now on my
way there.

                    SECOND MAN
What's to become of this place?

                         He indicates Scrooge's
                         office building. Bob
                         Cratchit shrugs
                         slightly; his interest
                         less than active.

                    CRATCHIT
To be pulled down, I've heard it said. A
new building to take its place. (A wan
smile.) A new age, sir--progress. The old
must, in its time, give way.

                    FIRST MAN
(Looking at the building.) Just as well,
if you ask me. A hulking old ruin. Well
past its time. If business is to be
encouraged, the old must make way for the
new. Yet it sometimes pains to see a place
so familiar disappear entirely, no matter
its history.

                    CRATCHIT
I am sure you are right, sir. (Tips his
hat.) My best wishes for the New Year.
Good day. (Turns to the Second Man.) Good
day to you, sir.

                    BOTH
Good day.

                         Cratchit resumes his
                         walk. The two men
                         watch him go.

FIRST MAN

A good man, that. Always wished he had
been my clerk. But he was too loyal by
half.

SECOND MAN

Indeed? I myself asked him on more than
one occasion to come clerk for me.

FIRST MAN

Is that so?

SECOND MAN

Much the same answer. (They begin to walk.)
As you say--too loyal by half. Especially
to such a miserly wretch as Scrooge.

FIRST MAN

Yes, but I would think he now has his
just reward.

SECOND MAN

Just so.

> They stop and look
> back on Scrooge's
> office building.

FIRST MAN

A sorry thing to be said of a man when the
passing of a building will be more greatly
mourned than he who occupied it.

SECOND MAN

(As they leave.) Just so, just so.

> The scene fades.
> Scrooge turns to the
> Third Spirit.

                    SCROOGE
I have seen enough, Spirit. (With
resignation.) Pray release me--since hope
is gone, what further merit to this
journey?

                    The Third Spirit
                    stands silent.

Spirit, hear me! I am not the man I was.
To what purpose do you haunt me still? Is
there no end to this torment?

                THIRD SPIRIT
One place more we yet must visit. Prepare,
Ebenezer Scrooge; the final scene awaits
us. Follow where I lead.

        SCENE 8
        The light fades on everything but
        Scrooge and the Third Spirit. The
        wind rises; a cold light builds
        around them. Shadows of great trees
        emerge from the darkness, a low
        ground fog swirls around their feet
        partly covering the indistinct low
        forms just now becoming visible.
        Scrooge must strain to see in this
        dim light.

                SCROOGE
This is the most fearful place of all.
Where be we now, Spirit?

                THIRD SPIRIT
A winter wood.

                SCROOGE
(Softly.) A dark place. It chills my soul.

THIRD SPIRIT

There is a colder place yet to come--and
still more dark.

> The Third Spirit
> steps forward and
> with slow
> deliberation points
> to the forms on the
> ground. Scrooge
> comes closer to see
> the exact place
> where the Spirit
> would have him look.
> The light becomes
> stronger in this
> isolated area. With
> mute horror Scrooge
> recognizes the
> specific object to
> which his eye has
> been directed.

SCROOGE

No . . . no. . . .

> His legs give out
> from under him; he is
> kneeling at his own
> grave.

THIRD SPIRIT

Do you read what name is carved upon the
stone?

SCROOGE

(Weakly.) I do, Spirit--I do . . . it is
mine. (Weaker still.) Mine. . . .

THIRD SPIRIT

There is no place more dark, more cold,
Ebenezer Scrooge--unless it be the soul of
the man who will not give to his fellow
creatures his compassion with a loving
heart. And in his lifetime it must be
done, for there is no reaching out from
here.

SCROOGE

(A pause and then more softly still.) Is
this to be my end? In this lonely and
forsaken spot? With no single token of
remembrance placed upon my grave? Is this,
Spirit, the final thing to be shown to me
this night?

> The Third Spirit has
> turned away from
> Scrooge and is silent.

(Stronger and more desperate.) So far from
all? Not one to mark my passing? Alone
. . . and forgotten?

> The Third Spirit
> remains as before.

(In a sudden burst of remorse.) Is there
no way that I may not come to this!? Speak,
I pray, if there is but one single shred
of hope for me! (With a pitiful resolve.)
I would not have this so!

> The sound of the
> rising wind is mixed
> with that of a great
> bell.

(With final desperation.) Spirit! (Echos
of his voice resound.) Spirit!!! Do not

leave me without a single word of comfort!
Tell me--if any pity remains in this dark
world--what I can--what I must do?!

                    THIRD SPIRIT
(From a great distance.) You have always
known the way . . . (his voice fades to a
ghostly sound which blends with the
falling wind) . . . E - B - E - N - E -
Z - E - R - S - C - R - O - O - G - E. . .

        SCENE 9
        Scrooge sinks to the floor weeping.
        All light fades. A steeple bell rings
        six times. Then another bell begins
        to chime, then another. But these are
        happier tones than those of the bells
        in Scrooge's visions. They are, in
        fact, the bells ringing in the
        Christmas morning. When the light
        returns, Scrooge is sitting in his
        own chair in his own room.

                    SCROOGE
(Coming out of the dream.) Tell me what I
must do . . . (He wakes with a start.)
Eh!? What? My own room . . . this is my
own room!

                              He rises, looks
                              around him and laughs
                              and starts to examine
                              every part of the
                              room to assure
                              himself that what he
                              sees and touches is
                              actually there.

My chair . . . my stove . . . my door! And
all just as it was. A miracle! It can be
nothing less! A miracle!!!

> His spirit and manner
> become more animated
> as he moves about the
> room. He goes to the
> window and throws it
> open. The bright
> winter sun streams in.

And the clear light of morning! (Tears of
joy.) A MIRACLE!!!

> At this point a young
> boy comes down the
> street. Seeing him,
> Scrooge leans out the
> window.

You there! Boy! Come here! (The boy stops
in surprise.) Yes, you!

                    BOY
Yes, sir?

                    SCROOGE
Tell me, lad, what day is this?

                    BOY
(Incredulous.) What day? What day!?

                    SCROOGE
Yes! Yes! What day! Speak out, boy. What
day is this!?

> A little of the old
> irascibleness returns,
> but with a touch more
> warmth in it.

Scene 9   101

                         BOY
But, sir! Everyone knows what day this
is. . . .

                       SCROOGE
Then for pity's sake tell me if what I
think is true. . . . Is this. . . . (He
almost hesitates to speak the blessed day's
name.) . . . Can this be. . . . <u>Christmas
Day</u>!?

                         BOY
Indeed, sir, no other!

                              Scrooge is stunned
                              into relieved silence.
                              Slowly the good news
                              of his reprieve dawns
                              on him. He is, in a
                              moment, transformed
                              into the new Scrooge.
                              The boy takes one
                              more look at the very
                              strange man and turns
                              to leave.

                       SCROOGE
Boy!

                         BOY
(Stopping.) Sir?

                       SCROOGE
Do ye know the butcher's shop at the end
of this street?

                         BOY
Oh, yes, sir. Know it well.

                       SCROOGE
Then--a moment, please. . . .

> From out the pocket
> of his dressinggown,
> he removes a small
> ragged purse. Opening
> it, he takes out two
> coins.

Go to that same shop and buy the biggest
goose there.

> He tosses one of the
> coins to the boy, who
> looks a little
> bewildered.

Wait! (Remembering.) The one in his front
window! I saw it but yesterday. An
extravagant fine bird, I thought--that's
the one I'd have!

                    BOY
Oh, yes, sir! I know the one you mean. The
one that's big as me!

                    SCROOGE
(To the world.) What an intelligent lad!
(To the boy.) Yes--yes, that is the one!!
And if you do it in the next five minutes,
you shall have this . . . (he holds up an
even larger coin) . . . for yourself!

                    BOY
(In utter disbelief.) Truly, sir!?

                    SCROOGE
My word upon it, boy!

                    BOY
Yes, sir! (Running off.) I'm almost there
and back again!

A remarkable boy! A remarkable boy! A
credit to the nation!

> There are three loud
> single knocks at the
> great locked door.
> The insistence of the
> sounds causes Scrooge
> to freeze in his
> tracks. It is a
> moment before he
> answers.

Who . . . who's there! (Pause.) Speak up!
Who's there!

> No answer. With some
> trepidation, he
> approaches the door,
> puts his ear to it
> and then, warily,
> unbolts and unlocks
> it. He throws it open
> only to find his
> beaming nephew
> standing there.

NEPHEW
The proverbial bad penny turns up for yet
another try.

> He quickly holds up
> his hand to the
> speechless Scrooge.

No quarrel, uncle. Peace. I just called
round this glorious morning to inquire
once more. . . .

                    SCROOGE
Nephew! My own dear boy! The one person in
all this world I most would see!

                         Scrooge grabs his
                         hand and arm, all but
                         dragging him into the
                         room. Quite naturally,
                         the nephew is
                         dumbfounded at this
                         greeting.

Come in, dear boy! Come in!

                    NEPHEW
Uncle? . . . uncle Ebenezer??

                    SCROOGE
Quite right. Your <u>uncle</u> Ebenezer. Oh, how
good to be called "uncle!" (Pushing him
into the large chair.) Do so again, dear
boy. Again.

                    NEPHEW
But I have <u>always</u> called you uncle . . .
uncle.

                    SCROOGE
(Blithely astounded.) Is that so?

                    NEPHEW
(Laughing now.) Indeed--uncle. (Slightly
suspicious.) Uncle . . . are you . . .
quite well?

                    SCROOGE
Eh?

                    NEPHEW
Do you feel . . . all right?

Scene 9   105

SCROOGE

Lord, bless ye, nephew--I'm in astounding
health! In the best of healths, thank'ee.
(With true concern.) And you? How do you
find yourself this finest of mornings?

NEPHEW

To be quite frank, uncle--a little
perplexed.

SCROOGE

Then be not so! For it is Christmas day,
and miracles--so they say--do happen at
that blessed time.

NEPHEW

And so I believe it--but never so much till
now, uncle.

> The nephew is quick
> to perceive that some
> marvelous change has
> taken place in
> Scrooge, but is wise
> enough not to question
> too closely its origin
> Outside in the street,
> the boy has returned
> with the great bird
> wrapped in brown
> paper, its feet
> hanging from the
> bottom. He taps at
> the window.

BOY

Sir?

SCROOGE

A moment, nephew. Some important business
to attend which will not keep.

> Scrooge is a continual
> surprize to his
> relative this strange
> morning. Scrooge goes
> to the window and
> opens it.

And have ye the requested bird, my lad?

                    BOY
The same, sir.

                    SCROOGE
Excellent! Excellent! And was the money I
gave thee sufficient to the purpose?

                    BOY
This left, sir. (Holding up a small coin.)
May I toss it up?

                    SCROOGE
Nay, child--keep it, keep it!

> This causes a rapid
> turning of the head
> of the nephew. Scrooge
> takes the other coin
> he promised the boy
> and tosses it down.

There's for your pains, hearty young
fellow!

> Catching the coin but
> almost dropping the
> bird.

                    BOY
Thank you, sir!

                    SCROOGE
(A thought strikes him.) Boy! Would you
consider the mating of those coins with
yet another?

                    BOY
Sir? (Beginning to be as amazed as the
nephew.)

                    SCROOGE
(Very clearly.) I said--would ye like a
shilling to match the ones you have?

                    BOY
Aye, sir--to be sure!

                    SCROOGE
Well, then, young sir, this other piece
. . . (holding up another coin from the
rapidly depleted purse) . . . is yours if
you will deliver the bird this very
morning as I direct.

                    BOY
I'm the man for the job!

                    SCROOGE
A fine reply! (To his nephew.) A
remarkably fine and apt reply, nephew.
This lad will go far, I predict.

                         He turns, tosses the
                         coin to the boy and
                         immediately closes
                         the window leaving
                         the boy, very puzzled,
                         standing in the street

And now, nephew, you must tell me the
whole story of. . . .

> The boy taps on the
> window again.

Eh?!

> A little of the old
> impatient Scrooge
> glimmers through. He
> opens the window and
> is surprized to see
> the boy.

What!? Still here?!

                    BOY
(Slight pause.) An address, sir?

                    SCROOGE
An address? An address?

                    BOY
Where . . . (he struggles with the bird)
should he be taken?

                    SCROOGE
(To his nephew.) What a fine head for
detail! This lad is sure to make the best
of business men! (Turns back to the boy.)
A humble appology, lad. To be sure, an
address, as you have wisely detected, is
an absolute necessity. The address is--can
you remember what I tell, or should I
write it down?

                    BOY
Oh, I'll remember well enough.

                    SCROOGE
Good . . . good! Then take that fine bird
to one Bob Cratchit of Petticoat Lane. Now,
do ye know the street?

Scene 9   109

BOY

Pass up and down it twice a day, I do.
Day in. Day out. For I live at the
farthest end of that same road.

SCROOGE

(Astounded at the cleverness of the lad
to be born on that particular street.)
The brightest of boys, nephew! He lives
on the very street needed! The future's
in good hands! Good hands!

> By now the nephew
> knows that not only
> has a miracle of
> great importance
> taken place, but that
> the change in Scrooge
> is not simply a
> superficial one.

NEPHEW

Most sure, uncle. (Slyly.) But then, I
always held you to be an excellent judge
of character.

SCROOGE

(Not perceiving the slight innuendo.) Eh?
Why, yes . . . yes. So I fancy myself to
be. An excellent judge of character--Bob
Cratchit being in my employ should be
proof enough of that.

> The boy has been
> waiting just in case
> there is something
> else he should know.

BOY

Sir? Will that be all?

                    SCROOGE
(Seeing he is still there.) Speed! All
speed, boy! Speed's the thing we want!

                    BOY
Yes, sir.

                    SCROOGE
Within the hour? A promise? (A thoughtful
slight pause.) Would ye like another coin?

                    BOY
(Starting to go.) No, sir.

                              He decides to leave
                              before the crazy old
                              gentleman has time to
                              reconsider.

A Merry Christmas!

                    SCROOGE
(Leaning far out of the window.) A Merry
Christmas! (The boy is gone, but Scrooge
likes the sound of the greeting.) A Merry
Christmas to all.

                              He closes the window
                              for the last time.
                              Scrooge has settled
                              very comfortably into
                              his new self.

What a morning--a trifle on the chilly
side . . . but what a fine new day it
promises to be!

                    NEPHEW
(Quietly.) Indeed, it does, uncle.

                    SCROOGE
Nephew. . . .

                              A slightly dark tone
                              enters into Scrooge's
                              voice.

                    NEPHEW
Yes, uncle?

                    SCROOGE
When the events are further off, I would
tell you all of the night I have just
past. A strange, but wonderful experience.

                    NEPHEW
(Not pushing in the least.) I would be
honored to hear it, uncle.

                    SCROOGE
I was borne by a cruel tide through a
world of darkness and bright light. But
now, safely home . . . (he looks about
himself with profound gratitude) . . . the
fever I suffered is past. (A slight
pause.) You see before you a man recovered
and in true health.

                    NEPHEW
Let me be so bold to say that the fever,
uncle Ebenezer, consummed you for many a
year before last night. (Smiles.) But, sure
enough, what I see now before me is a most
well man.

                    SCROOGE
I pray you be proved right, dear boy.

NEPHEW

(A glint in his eye.) I too am a good
judge of character, uncle; a family trait,
I'd be willing to wager.

SCROOGE

(In an almost playful mood.) Oh, would you
now?

> They have become, in
> the shortest while,
> old cronies as well
> as blood relatives.

NEPHEW

I would--and win for sure! (They both
laugh.) But, now, uncle, no more delay--
get your best frock coat--your finest
muffler--that ancient monument you
respectfully call a hat, which, by the by,
we will retire tomorrow morning in favor
of one more fitting to your new estate.

SCROOGE

And what would that be, nephew?

NEPHEW

Why--the merriest gentleman in London Town!

SCROOGE

Just so, just so.

NEPHEW

And now, Ebenezer Scrooge. . . . Prepare!

> His voice has become
> impressively
> commanding. There is
> almost a note of the

voices of the Spirits
in his tone.

SCROOGE
Prepare? For what?

NEPHEW
(The brightest of smiles.) <u>To</u> <u>come</u> <u>home</u>
<u>with</u> <u>me</u> <u>for</u> <u>Christmas</u> <u>dinner</u>!

Scrooge hesitates; a
whole new world
presents itself to
him.

SCROOGE
(A pause, then.) And why not!?

Throwing off his
dressinggown and
night cap, he dresses
quickly. The nephew
opens the door as if
for a monarch and
goes out into the
hall-way. Just before
going completely out
the door, Scrooge
stops and looks back
in, giving the room a
searching look.

A dream? . . . Perhaps.

He shrugs and then
looks up as if to see
beyond the dark
ceiling.

Jacob!? Jacob. . . .

A pause.

Many thanks, old friend. . . . (He smiles.)
. . . Peace.

                    NEPHEW
(Now outside the house.) Come along, uncle.
The new age waits!

                    SCROOGE
(Shaking himself from his reverie.) Eh!?
Yes. . . . Yes, indeed, my boy. Lead on.
Lead on, and I'll keep pace.

         SCENE 10
         As Scrooge exits the room turns
         leaving the two men on the front
         steps of Scrooge's house.

(Looking up.) A fine morning.

                    NEPHEW
As you say, uncle. A fine morning to a
fine new day. (Stepping into the street.)
Uncle Ebenezer . . . look!

                    SCROOGE
Eh!?

                    NEPHEW
(Pointing.) See who comes down the street?

                    SCROOGE
Why . . . to be sure, it's Bob Cratchit!

                    NEPHEW
And his whole brood in tow.

SCROOGE

(Struck by a thought.) Nephew! Step back into the alleyway.

NEPHEW

What?

SCROOGE

Do it! Do it, my boy! Hide yourself.

NEPHEW

Uncle? Do you feel all right?

SCROOGE

I do! Never better! But I would like to play the smallest of pranks on Bob there. Go to, boy! Go! You'll see.

NEPHEW

(Smiling, he steps into the alleyway.) Very well, uncle.

SCROOGE

Good! Good. (Over his shoulder to his hidden nephew.) Now--watch.

> The Cratchit family enters the square before Scrooge's House. They are engaged in spirited conversation. Scrooge steps forward and blocks their passage.

(Putting on his old character.) Bob Cratchit!

BOB CRATCHIT
(Startled.) Mr. Scrooge. . . ! (Quickly recovering himself.) A good morning to you, sir.·

SCROOGE
(Looking up.) A tolerable day, sir . . . tolerable. It could be a worse one, I think.

BOB CRATCHIT
. . . Yes . . . yes . . . it could be. . . .

SCROOGE
(Cutting him off.) And, where, Mr. Cratchit, do you and your family go?

TINY TIM
To church, sir.

SCROOGE
Eh!?

TINY TIM
It's Christmas morn.

SCROOGE
(Nodding in a noncommittal way.) So I've been informed, lad. So I've been told.

> All stand in silence for a brief moment. Finally Bob Cratchit breaks the impasse.

BOB CRATCHIT
Well, sir. (Tips his hat.) May we wish you a very good day.

                              They all cooly assent
                              and begin their
                              journey again.

                    SCROOGE
(Almost sharply, but not quite.) Anything
unusual happen this morning, Mr. Cratchit?

                  BOB CRATCHIT
(Turning back.) Well, sir, now that you
mention it, something did.

                    SCROOGE
So!?

                  BOB CRATCHIT
We were delivered a great fine bird,
dressed for baking. A mistake, I thought,
on the boy's part who brought it. Although
he said it was indeed meant for our house.
(Still puzzled by the event.) A mystery,
sir.

                    SCROOGE
(Quietly.) No mystery, sir.

                  BOB CRATCHIT
Pardon?

                    SCROOGE
And no mistake either.

                  BOB CRATCHIT
(More puzzled than ever.) Sir?

                    SCROOGE
Be ye hard of hearing? I said--no mistake!
For you see, Bob--I sent that bird!

                              The whole family stand
                              with open mouths.

TINY TIM
(Innocently disbelieving.) It couldn't
have been you, sir?

SCROOGE
But, my boy, it was! Me. . . . (He is now
all smiles having revealed his new self.)
No one else.

MRS. CRATCHIT
(Thinking the old man to have gone mad.)
Bob. . . ?

BOB CRATCHIT
You, Mr. Scrooge?! You sent it?!!

SCROOGE
And late it is, Bob . . . many years.
(Stepping closer to the family.) But not
too late, I hope.

                    At this moment the
                    nephew steps out of
                    his hiding place.

NEPHEW
Be not amazed, Bob Cratchit.

BOB CRATCHIT
Sir? Forgive me, but I most certainly am.

NEPHEW
A miraculous transformation. This, ladies
and gentlemen, is my uncle Ebenezer as I
found him this morning. Another proof, I'd
say, of the marvelous nature of the season.

BOB CRATCHIT
I . . . I. . . .

NEPHEW
(Holding up a finger to his lips.) Ah! No
questions, my good man. (Softly but
emphatically.) Accept--what--you--see. I
assure you . . . the vision is real.

SCROOGE
What do I pay ye, man!?

                        Bob Cratchit opens
                        his mouth to speak
                        but no sound emerges.

(Quickly going on.) Well, it's not enough
for a growing family such as this. (He
steps into their midst.) First thing
tomorrow, sir, enter your new wage in the
ledger. And make it double the sum now
drawn. . . .

BOB CRATCHIT
Mr. Scrooge. . . .

SCROOGE
(Not paying him any attention.) No! Make
it triple. And well deserved for the many
years of good and faithful service to the
firm.

MRS. CRATCHIT
Oh, Bob!

                        She gives him a great
                        embrace. The children
                        also become
                        increasingly
                        animated. Tiny Tim
                        comes forward and
                        tugs at Scrooge's
                        sleeve until he gains
                        attention.

SCROOGE
Eh? What is it lad?

TINY TIM
May I ask you a question, Mr. Scrooge?

SCROOGE
A question? And what's to prevent you doing so. Ask away, my boy, ask away.

TINY TIM
Would you like to come with us to our church? It's a very nice place to spend a Christmas morning.

> Scrooge is taken aback by the boy's simple and straightforward generosity. He hesitates, then turns to his nephew who smilingly nods that he should accept the offer.

SCROOGE
Well--if ye'll have me, I'd be very pleased to come.

BOB CRATCHIT
(Now fully recovered.) With the greatest of pleasures.

SCROOGE
Do you mind, nephew?

NEPHEW
Not if you promise to come round when the service is done.

Scene 10   121

TINY TIM

And after a piece of my mum's plum
pudding!

NEPHEW

And . . . <u>after</u> a piece of your mum's plum
pudding!

SCROOGE

You have my word.

BOB CRATCHIT

(Looking at his watch.) Ah! Come, we've
only minutes to spare. Wouldn't do to be
late on this day of days.

> They all begin to
> leave. Scrooge and
> Tiny Tim, who has
> taken Scrooge's
> hand, are the last in
> the procession.

NEPHEW

(Calling after them.) A merry Christmas to
you all.

ALL

And the same to you and yours.

TINY TIM

He did, papa!

BOB CRATCHIT

Who did, Tim? And did what?

TINY TIM

God did--He blessed us. He blessed us--
everyone!

In high spirits they
leave. The nephew is
left alone as the
light fades on the
scene.

FINIS

The Canticle of Christmas Present

arranged by George Pinney

Peep & crisp & even. Dame, what makes your ducks to die, ducks to die,
La_____ la_   Dame, what makes your

ducks to die? Dame, what makes your ducks to die, on Christ-mas day in the
ducks to die, ducks to die,   ducks to die?   Dame, what makes your

morn - ing?   Their wings are cut   they   can-not fly, their
ducks to die on Christ-mas day in the wings are cut & they   can-not fly,

wings are cut they can-not fly;   wings are cut   they   can-not fly on
can - not fly,   can-not fly; their wings are cut & they   can-not fly on

Christmas day in the   E-be-ne-zer Scrooge!!!

transcribed by Tom Pallen.